my **revisi⊕n** notes

AQA AS
GEOGRAPHY

Michael Raw

HODDER
EDUCATION

With thanks to all the students whose valuable feedback helped develop this book.

Hodder Education, an Hachette UK company, 338 Euston Road, London NW1 3BH

Orders

Bookpoint Ltd, 130 Milton Park, Abingdon, Oxfordshire OX14 4SB

tel: 01235 827827

fax: 01235 400401

e-mail: education@bookpoint.co.uk

Lines are open 9.00 a.m.–5.00 p.m., Monday to Saturday, with a 24-hour message answering service. You can also order through the Hodder Education website: www.hoddereducation.co.uk

© Michael Raw 2012

ISBN 978-1-4441-5250-0

First printed 2012

Impression number 5 4 3 2

Year 2017 2016 2015 2014 2013 2012

Cover photo reproduced by permission of ANK/Fotolia

Typeset by Dianne Shaw

Printed in India

Hachette UK's policy is to use papers that are natural, renewable and recyclable products and made from wood grown in sustainable forests. The logging and manufacturing processes are expected to conform to the environmental regulations of the country of origin.

P01951

Get the most from this book

Everyone has to decide his or her own revision strategy, but it is essential to review your work, learn it and test your understanding. These Revision Notes will help you to do that in a planned way, topic by topic. Use this book as the cornerstone of your revision and don't hesitate to write in it — personalise your notes and check your progress by ticking off each section as you revise.

☑ Tick to track your progress

Use the revision planner on pages 4 and 5 to plan your revision, topic by topic. Tick each box when you have:

● revised and understood a topic

● tested yourself

● practised the exam questions and gone online to check your answers and complete the quick quizzes

You can also keep track of your revision by ticking off each topic heading in the book. You may find it helpful to add your own notes as you work through each topic.

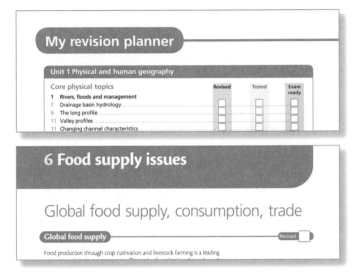

Features to help you succeed

Examiner's tips and summaries

Throughout the book there are tips from the examiner to help you boost your final grade.

Summaries provide advice on how to approach each topic in the exams, and suggest other things you might want to mention to gain those valuable extra marks.

Typical mistake

The examiner identifies the typical mistakes candidates make and explains how you can avoid them.

Definitions and key words

Clear, concise definitions of essential key terms are provided on the page where they appear.

Key words from the specification are highlighted in bold for you throughout the book.

Exam practice

Practice exam questions are provided for each topic. Use them to consolidate your revision and practise your exam skills.

Now test yourself

These short, knowledge-based questions provide the first step in testing your learning. Answers are at the back of the book.

Check your understanding

Use these questions at the end of each section to make sure that you have understood every topic. Answers are at the back of the book.

Online

Go online to check your answers to the exam questions and try out the extra quick quizzes at **www.therevisionbutton.co.uk/myrevisionnotes**

My revision planner

Exam practice answers and quick quizzes at **www.therevisionbutton.co.uk/myrevisionnotes**

Countdown to my exams

6–8 weeks to go

- Start by looking at the specification — make sure you know exactly what material you need to revise and the style of the examination. Use the revision planner on pages 4 and 5 to familiarise yourself with the topics.
- Organise your notes, making sure you have covered everything on the specification. The revision planner will help you to group your notes into topics.
- Work out a realistic revision plan that will allow you time for relaxation. Set aside days and times for all the subjects that you need to study, and stick to your timetable.
- Set yourself sensible targets. Break your revision down into focused sessions of around 40 minutes, divided by breaks. These Revision Notes organise the basic facts into short, memorable sections to make revising easier.

Revised ☐

4–6 weeks to go

- Read through the relevant sections of this book and refer to the examiner's tips, examiner's summaries, typical mistakes and key terms. Tick off the topics as you feel confident about them. Highlight those topics you find difficult and look at them again in detail.
- Test your understanding of each topic by working through the 'Now test yourself' and 'Check your understanding' questions in the book. Look up the answers at the back of the book.
- Make a note of any problem areas as you revise, and ask your teacher to go over these in class.
- Look at past papers. They are one of the best ways to revise and practise your exam skills. Write or prepare planned answers to the exam practice questions provided in this book. Check your answers online and try out the extra quick quizzes at **www.therevisionbutton.co.uk/ myrevisionnotes**
- Try different revision methods. For example, you can make notes using mind maps, spider diagrams or flash cards.
- Track your progress using the revision planner and give yourself a reward when you have achieved your target.

Revised ☐

One week to go

- Try to fit in at least one more timed practice of an entire past paper and seek feedback from your teacher, comparing your work closely with the mark scheme.
- Check the revision planner to make sure you haven't missed out any topics. Brush up on any areas of difficulty by talking them over with a friend or getting help from your teacher.
- Attend any revision classes put on by your teacher. Remember, he or she is an expert at preparing people for examinations.

Revised ☐

The day before the examination

- Flick through these Revision Notes for useful reminders, for example the examiner's tips, examiner's summaries, typical mistakes and key terms.
- Check the time and place of your examination.
- Make sure you have everything you need — extra pens and pencils, tissues, a watch, bottled water, sweets.
- Allow some time to relax and have an early night to ensure you are fresh and alert for the examinations.

Revised ☐

My exams

AS Geography Unit 1

Date: ....

Time: ....

Location: ....

AS Geography Unit 2

Date: ....

Time: ....

Location: ....

1 Rivers, floods and management

Drainage basin hydrology

Drainage basin hydrological cycle

Revised ☐

A **drainage basin** is the area drained by a river and its tributaries. It is a natural system, with inputs, flows, and stores of water and sediment. Each drainage basin has its own distinctive hydrology, with variable inputs of precipitation and outputs of water through evaporation, transpiration and river flow. In the long term there is a balance between inputs and outputs of water. This **water balance** is summarised as:

precipitation = evaporation + transpiration + river flow ± storage

Water is stored in porous rocks, soils, peat and vegetation. During years of low precipitation storage is depleted. Periods of above-average precipitation increase storage levels.

Factors affecting river discharge

Revised ☐

River discharge is the volume of water (measured in m^3) that flows in a river channel over a set period of time (usually one second). Many factors influence discharge. They are broadly divided into two groups (Table 1.1): fixed and variable physical properties of drainage basins.

Table 1.1 Factors influencing river discharge

Fixed physical properties of drainage basins	
Geology	Permeable rocks, such as chalk, store most precipitation and release it slowly. This reduces extremes of discharge. Impermeable rocks have the opposite effect.
Slopes	Water moves slowly across/through gentle slopes to streams and rivers. In upland drainage basins steep slopes result in rapid water movement, with high discharge maintained for short periods.
Soils	Impermeable clay soils cause rapid runoff and higher discharge.
Drainage density	Drainage density is the average length of stream channel per km^2. Where drainage density is high, surface and subsurface water is transferred quickly to river channels, increasing discharge levels.
Vegetation	Dense vegetation intercepts a large proportion of precipitation. Water stored on vegetation surfaces is lost to evaporation and soil water is absorbed by plant roots. Vegetation also slows the movement of water to rivers. Drainage basins with sparse vegetation cover experience higher peak discharges than well-vegetated basins.
Land use	Areas with man-made drainage (e.g. cropland, towns and cities) and artificial impermeable surfaces (e.g. towns and cities) promote rapid runoff and high peak discharge. Forestry plantations have the opposite effect.
Basin shape	Roughly circular drainage basins have higher peak discharges than more elongated basins.

Variable physical properties of drainage basins and storm characteristics	
Antecedent soil moisture	If soils are already saturated or frozen (i.e. in winter) they shed water rapidly and discharge is high.
Precipitation intensity	High-intensity precipitation in thunderstorms may exceed the soil's infiltration capacity, causing rapid runoff and high discharge.
Precipitation type	Snow and ice take variable lengths of time to thaw and contribute to discharge. Rapid snowmelt may produce exceptionally high discharges sustained for several days.

Storm hydrographs

Revised

A **storm hydrograph** is a chart that shows how discharge of a stream or river responds to a period of precipitation (see Figure 1.1). Precipitation and discharge are recorded at 15-minute or hourly intervals. The main features of storm hydrographs are:

- A **rising limb** — the increase in discharge in response to precipitation. The more rapid the response (i.e. the more quickly rain gets into the river) the steeper the rising limb.
- **Peak flow** — the maximum discharge in response to a precipitation event.
- A **falling limb** — when discharge declines after peak flow.
- The **lag time** — the difference between the time of maximum precipitation and that of peak discharge.
- **Stormflow** — the proportion of total discharge contributed by the precipitation event.
- **Base flow** — the proportion of total discharge contributed by water stored in permeable rocks, soils, vegetation, etc.

> **Typical mistake**
>
> Over a year inputs of precipitation to a drainage basin are rarely balanced by outputs. Some water is always entering or leaving storage.

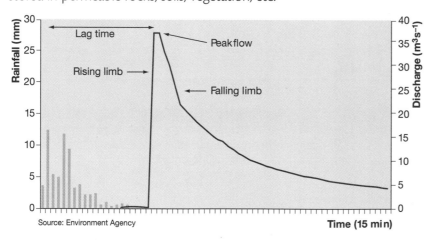

Figure 1.1 Hydrograph for the Upper Calder River, 6 July 2006

> **Examiner's tip**
>
> You need to be able to interpret storm hydrographs and, from the pattern of discharge, infer the fixed properties of drainage basins and the risk of flooding.

Streams and rivers that respond rapidly to precipitation and have high (but often short-lived) peak flows are described as **flashy** (see Figure 1.1). The flood risk is particularly high along such streams and rivers.

Flowpaths

Revised

Rain follows one of two paths as it flows to streams and rivers:

- infiltration into the soil and movement to streams and rivers via **throughflow** and **groundwater flow** (see Figure 1.2)
- **overland flow**, across the ground surface.

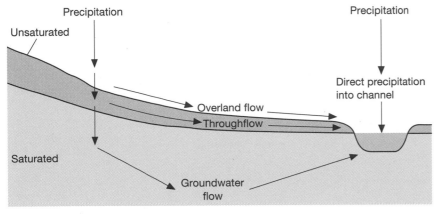

Figure 1.2 Flowpaths to streams and rivers

It is argued that the path followed by rainwater depends on the soil's infiltration capacity (i.e. the maximum rate at which soil can absorb rain). If rainfall intensity is less than infiltration capacity throughflow will dominate, while the opposite situation produces overland flow. Conversely, some experts believe that all rainfall, regardless of its intensity, infiltrates the soil. This results in a rise in the soil **water table**. Eventually the water table reaches the surface causing puddling and **saturated overland flow**.

Now test yourself

1 (a) What is the water balance?
   (b) Explain the role of storage in the water balance.

2 List all the factors you can think of that influence river discharge.

3 Why do 'flashy' rivers often present a severe flood hazard?

4 Sketch two storm hydrographs to show the response of a river draining (a) a porous chalk drainage basin and (b) an impermeable clay drainage basin. Add labels to explain the main features of the hydrographs.

Answers on p. 119

The long profile

The long profile of a river describes its longitudinal cross-section from source to mouth. Most rivers are concave in long profile. This is known as a **graded profile**, with a relatively steep (but short) section near the source (often in the uplands), and a much longer section with gentle gradients in the lowlands and towards the mouth.

Changing processes   Revised ☐

The processes of erosion, transport and deposition (and their relative importance), together with the characteristics of the sediment load, vary with distance downstream.

Erosion

Erosion occurs mainly in the upper parts of drainage basins where steep slopes and high peak flows provide surplus energy. There are four principal fluvial erosion processes: abrasion (or corrasion), hydraulic action, cavitation and solution (or corrosion).

Abrasion is mainly caused by the transport of **bedload**. High energy levels allow streams and rivers to transport coarse rock particles that scour the channel bed and undercut channel banks. Abrasion, together with the collision of bedload particles, results in the **attrition** and downstream rounding and fining of river sediments.

Hydraulic action describes the dragging force of flowing water, dislodging particles of sand and silt from the bed and banks of stream channels. It is most effective where channels are formed from incoherent materials such as sand and gravel.

Cavitation occurs when air bubbles implode in fissures and cracks in channel banks. The tiny shock waves they create weaken the banks and contribute to collapse.

Solution is the chemical action of water, which dissolves carbonate rocks such as chalk and limestone.

Sediment transport

Load is the term used to describe all the sediment (and dissolved minerals) transported by a stream or river, ranging in size from boulders and cobbles to pebbles, sand, silt and clay. Sediments of different size of **calibre** are moved variously by **traction** and **saltation**, and in **suspension** and in **solution** (Table 1.2).

Table 1.2 Types of river sediment and their transport

Type of load	Sediments	Transport processes and location
Bedload	Coarse particles: boulders, cobbles and pebbles.	Mainly occurs upstream where river channels are dominated by coarse sediments. Particles slide and roll along the channel during high discharge.
Suspended load	Fine particles such as sand, silt and clay.	Occurs in all parts of a river's course. Silt and clay are entrained at high discharge and transported in suspension. Sand is transported by saltation, i.e. bounced along the channel bed.
Solution load	Dissolved minerals from rocks such as chalk and carboniferous limestone.	Occurs in all parts of a river's course. Minerals are transported in solution. This type of transport occurs continuously, regardless of energy levels.

Hjulström's curve

A river's ability to erode and transport particles of a given size is known as its **competence**. Hjulström's curve (Figure 1.3) summarises the relationship between river erosion, transport and deposition, and flow velocity and particle size.

A critical speed is required to remove and transport particles of a given size; this is the **critical erosion velocity**. Coarse particles (cobbles, pebbles) need lots of energy and therefore high flow velocities to get them moving. Fine particles (silt, clay) are also only transported at high velocities. This is because they stick together, bonded by tiny electrical charges. In contrast, sand-sized particles have relatively low erosion velocities. This is due to the loose and incoherent nature of sand and its small mass.

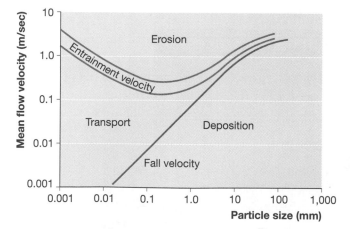

Figure 1.3 Hjulström's curve

The lower curve in Figure 1.3 shows the velocities needed for particles to settle out of suspension. It tells us that:

● coarse particles soon come to rest as flow speeds dip below the critical erosion velocity

● clay particles settle out of suspension only at very low velocities

These differences between critical erosion velocities and depositional velocities of particles have implications for sediment transport:

> **Typical mistake**
>
> Erosion includes both the abrasion (scouring) of river channels by bedload and also the removal of loose, unconsolidated materials such as sand and gravel. All three fluvial processes — erosion, transport and deposition — are found everywhere in a river's course.

Exam practice answers and quick quizzes at **www.therevisionbutton.co.uk/myrevisionnotes**

- coarse particles are in transit for relatively brief periods around peak discharge and are therefore likely to travel only short distances
- fine particles, once entrained, will be transported long distances. The selective removal of fine particles from upland streams is one reason why boulders and cobbles dominate stream channels in the uplands

> **Examiner's tip**
>
> The relationships between river energy and erosion, transport and deposition are crucial to understanding fluvial processes and landforms.

Valley profiles

Valley profiles and downstream changes
Revised

River valleys vary in cross-sectional and long-sectional shape. The contrasts are most obvious between upland and lowland valleys. Upland valleys have typically deep, narrow and V-shaped cross-sections. These characteristics are largely explained by steep gradients, which cause rivers to **erode vertically** and incise their valleys. When V-shaped valleys are *meandering*, they have **interlocking spurs**. In long-section, upland valleys are steep, uneven and interrupted at frequent intervals by waterfalls and rapids.

Lowland valleys have wider and shallower cross-sections. Valley floors are often extensive, flat and occupied by floodplains. In long-section, gradients are relatively gentle, and the long profile is smooth. These characteristic features reflect the different processes operating in the lowlands, especially **lateral erosion** caused by the endless shifting of meanders across the floodplain.

Potential and kinetic energy
Revised

The work of rivers, eroding the land and transporting water and sediment, requires energy. The amount of energy available depends on:
- the vertical distance to sea level at any point on a river's course (**potential energy**)
- the volume and velocity of flow

As rivers flow they convert potential energy to **kinetic energy** and perform work (e.g. erosion and sediment transport). On average 95% of kinetic energy is spent overcoming the internal friction of water and the frictional drag of the channel. The remainder is expended on erosion and the transport of the sediment load. However, this occurs only at high flow, when rivers have surplus energy.

> **Examiner's tip**
>
> Be aware that the potential energy available to a river can vary over short distances. For example, a sudden steepening of the channel caused by a change in geology increases potential energy which is converted into kinetic energy and erosion.

Changing channel characteristics

Channel cross profiles
Revised

In their valleys, rivers flow in channels defined by the bed and enclosing banks. The most important channel cross profile shape is **bankfull**, when discharge just reaches the top of the banks. At bankfull (a) the channel contains the maximum volume of water, (b) the river has the greatest energy, and (c) the river has maximum efficiency. Bankfull discharge determines the shape of the channel in cross-section. Like those of valleys, the cross-sections of river channels have a number of distinctive features.

Wetted perimeter and hydraulic radius

The **hydraulic radius** is the ratio of the bankfull cross-sectional area of a channel to its **wetted perimeter**. Wetted perimeter is the length of the channel bed and banks in cross-section that is in contact with the water at bankfull. The higher the value of the hydraulic radius, the more efficient the channel for transporting water.

Roughness and efficiency

Mountain streams, with wide, rough, shallow channels and coarse bedloads lose a great deal of energy to friction and are highly inefficient (low hydraulic radius). In contrast, smooth, deep channels with fine bedload provide little frictional resistance to flow. With minimal energy loss, flow in these channels is highly efficient (high hydraulic radius). As a result the river has more energy to expend on erosion and transport. Generally, river channels become more efficient with increasing distance downstream.

> **Typical mistake**
>
> Failure to realise that most river erosion and transport occurs on just one or two days a year, when rivers are at bankfull discharge.

> **Examiner's tip**
>
> Examiners look for an understanding that rivers are energy systems and that potential energy, derived from gradient and discharge, is converted to kinetic energy and work (erosion, transport).

Landforms of fluvial erosion and deposition

As rivers expend energy through erosion and transport they shape the landscape through distinctive erosional and depositional landforms.

Erosional landforms
Revised

Pot holes

In upland river channels of solid rock, the uneven bed causes turbulent, eddying flow. Pebbles trapped in eddies and vortices abrade circular holes (**pot holes**) in the river bed. Over time, the pot holes merge, lowering the river bed.

Waterfalls and rapids

Geological structure and past erosional events (e.g. glaciation) create abrupt changes in channel gradient and lead to the development of **waterfalls** and **rapids**. Steep, almost vertical rock steps produce waterfalls; more gently inclined resistant rocks that steepen and roughen the channel result in rapids. Waterfalls often form where:

- a band of resistant rock crosses a river channel; weaker underlying rock is eroded, undermining the resistant rock band which eventually collapses, maintaining the steep profile and retreating upstream

- a fault line creates a sudden change in rock type and triggers a similar sequence of events to that described above

- a river flows across a major structural boundary (e.g. the edge of a plateau) or an erosional feature such as a glacial valley

Meanders

Meanders are sinuous, wave-like river channels formed by both erosional and depositional processes. Approximately 80% of river channels are classed as meandering.

Meandering channels most commonly occur where:

● channel banks comprise coherent silt and clay, and

● the channel gradient is moderately steep so that the river has sufficient power to erode its banks

A secondary flow occurs within meanders, known as **helical flow** (see Figure 1.4). Helical flow is a corkscrew-like motion that simultaneously transfers water downstream and across the channel. A surface current moves across the river, elevating the water on the outside of the meander and undercutting the steep outer bank. This surface current is complemented by a return current close to the river bed directed at the inner bank. The return current is responsible for deposition on the inner bank and the formation of a convex **point bar**. Erosion on the outer bank and deposition on the inner bank cause meanders to migrate slowly across the valley floor. In doing so, they erode and widen the valley where they meet the valley slopes and are instrumental in the formation of **floodplains**.

Typical mistake

It is simplistic to explain point bars by reference to slower flow velocities on the inner bank of meanders. Deposition and point bar growth must be linked to helical flow.

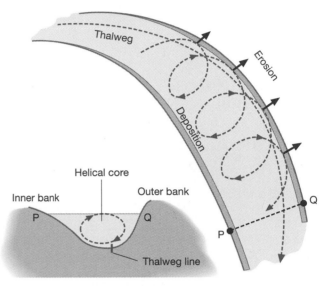

Figure 1.4 Helical flow in a meander

Depositional landforms   Revised

Braided channels

Braided channels are multiple-thread channels, comprising two or more channels divided by bars and islands. Channel division is caused by the deposition of sediment within the channel. Braiding results from a combination of:

● excessive bedload due to poorly vegetated surfaces and abundant coarse debris often derived from glaciation or volcanic eruptions

● banks of gravels and sand, which are easily eroded and cause localised overloading of rivers with coarse sediment

● high and variable discharge, with high peak flows, often associated in glaciated regions with meltwater

● steep channel gradients

Braiding suggests that a river cannot transport its sediment load in a single channel. Deposition within the channel (i.e. **aggradation**) steepens the channel gradient and restores the river's competence to transport its load.

Floodplains

Most lowland rivers occupy broad valley floors or floodplains. Floodplains are the result of both river erosion and deposition. Lateral erosion and the downstream migration of meanders widen the valley. Fluvial deposition infills the valley with **alluvium** (silt, sand and gravel). This involves two processes: lateral accretion and vertical accretion.

- **Lateral accretion** mainly comprises point bars and channel sediments, abandoned as the river shifts its course through lateral erosion. These deposits are often coarse (i.e. sand and gravel).
- **Vertical accretion** occurs when floodwater spills out of the channel and spreads across the valley floor. Deposited sediment consists of silt and clay transported as suspended load.

Levees

Levees are low ridges of alluvium that run parallel to and flank both sides of river channels. They form when water spills out of the channel at bankfull and quickly loses energy. Coarse sediment (e.g. sand) is deposited nearest the channel and, over many years, builds up to form levees.

Deltas

Along some coastlines, the volume of sediment deposited by rivers is too large to be removed by wave and tidal action. Under these conditions a **delta** of river-deposited sediment builds out into the sea. Deltas have great variations in planform, reflecting the influence of fluvial, wave and tidal controls.

Deltas comprise two morphological elements:

- a delta front (the shoreline and the gently sloping offshore zone)
- a delta plain that forms an extensive lowland made up of active and abandoned channels known as **distributaries**

Delta front shape is determined by the relative effectiveness of fluvial, tidal and wave processes. The Mississippi is the only major delta almost solely determined in shape by sediment deposition by distributary channels. It has undergone very little modification by tidal and wave processes. Where waves have more energy, a smooth arcuate shoreline is developed through the transport and deposition of river sediment by longshore currents (e.g. Nile Delta). Coasts with strong tidal scour have delta fronts dominated by ridges, channels and islands (e.g. Ganges–Brahmaputra Delta).

> **Examiner's tip**
>
> You need to demonstrate an understanding that the formation of features such as braids, meanders, floodplains and deltas is complex, each involving a range of factors and processes.

Rejuvenation

Processes of rejuvenation Revised

If the energy available to a river increases, some of this surplus energy is expended on erosion. The resulting change in the energy system which triggers renewed erosion is known as **rejuvenation**. Rejuvenation has two possible causes:

- an increase in discharge (e.g. climatic change leading to higher rainfall, melting glaciers and icefields)
- a change in **base level** (e.g. a lowering of sea level, **tectonic uplift**, **isostatic uplift**)

Rejuvenation creates a number of distinctive landforms, including knickpoints, river terraces and incised meanders.

Landforms of rejuvenation

Revised ☐

Knickpoints

Rivers have long profiles that are graded to sea level (or to their confluence with larger rivers). If sea level falls (or the principal river incises its channel) the river has a steeper gradient and adjusts by cutting down to the new base level. This process starts at sea level (or at a confluence) and progresses upstream. Where the new graded profile intersects the old, an abrupt change of gradient develops. This feature is called a **knickpoint**. Sometimes waterfalls and rapids are sited at knickpoints.

River terraces

Renewed erosion may cause a river to incise its channel into its floodplain. If this occurs rapidly, remnants of the original floodplain may be left abandoned as terraces along the edges of the valley. **River terraces** that result from rejuvenation are usually paired (i.e. at the same height) along either side of a valley.

Incised meanders

Meanders become incised when a rejuvenated river cuts vertically through its floodplain and into solid bedrock. There are two types of **incised meander**: intrenched and ingrown. Intrenched **meanders** occur where downcutting is rapid and there is little erosion and weathering of valley slopes. Ingrown meanders develop where there is a slower rate of downcutting and where valley slope decline is more significant. **Tectonic uplift** may accelerate the process of incision (e.g. uplift of the Colorado Plateau and the deep incision of intrenched meanders on the San Juan River, Utah).

> **Typical mistake**
>
> River energy systems are not static. Changes in climate and base level mean that they are constantly in a state of flux.

> **Tectonic uplift** occurs as a result of internal earth movements such as faulting and folding. Isostatic uplift occurs when deglaciation 'unloads' ice from the land, causing the land surface to rise vertically.

Now test yourself

5 (a) What is mean by a river's load? (b) Name three types of load and explain how they are influenced by a river's energy levels.

6 What is bankfull discharge and why is it important?

7 Draw annotated cross-sections to show the main features of (a) V-shaped valleys, (b) floodplains.

8 Explain how the formation of floodplains involves both river erosion and deposition.

9 Draw a cross-section of (a) an efficient and (b) an inefficient river. Which channel has the larger hydraulic radius value?

10 Why do some rivers have braided channels?

11 Draw a diagram showing the long (graded) profile of a river to explain the formation of knickpoints.

Answers on p. 119

Physical and human causes of flooding and the impact of floods

River floods occur when river discharge exceeds bankfull capacity. Excess water then spills out of the channel and inundates the valley floor. Floods are caused by a number of physical and human factors.

Physical causes

- Heavy precipitation. High-intensity precipitation associated with thunderstorms creates **flash floods** (e.g. Boscastle 2004). Prolonged, heavy precipitation over several days or weeks causes **slow floods** (e.g. Pakistan 2010).
- Rapid movement of surface and subsurface water into stream and river channels, giving short duration, high peak flows. Factors that promote rapid runoff of precipitation include: steep slopes, impermeable rocks and soils, lack of vegetation cover.
- Snowmelt. Sudden thaws may melt several weeks of accumulated snow.

Human causes

- Land use changes that accelerate runoff, e.g. urbanisation, deforestation, land drainage.
- Siltation of river channels because of soil erosion and subsequent aggradation that reduces the channel capacity.

Location of areas of high risk in MEDCs and LEDCs

Levels of flood risk depend on two factors: (1) **exposure,** i.e. the magnitude and frequency of flood events and the number of people living in flood-prone areas; (2) **vulnerability,** i.e. the ability of a society to protect itself from floods. Flood risks are high where one or more of the following conditions are found:

- proximity to upland areas where extreme precipitation frequently occurs, where runoff is rapid and where there is snow cover for part of the year
- floodplains — flat, low-lying valley floors which act as temporary stores for floodwater
- populations living at high densities on floodplains and valley floors

Populations who are poorly prepared for flood events increase the level of risk. Wealthy societies are well prepared, investing in flood protection schemes such as dams, levees, relief channels and reafforestation of catchments.

> **Typical mistake**
>
> The assumption that floods are simply caused by heavy and prolonged precipitation.

> **Examiner's tip**
>
> Understanding that river floods usually result from a combination of physical and human factors, and that the relative importance of these factors in specific floods events is often debatable.

> **Case study** | **Indus Valley (Pakistan)**
>
> The disastrous floods in Pakistan in 2010 underlined the high flood risk in much of the country. Risks are high because:
> - much of central and southern Pakistan is lowland, comprising vast alluvial plains drained by the Indus and its tributaries and occupied by millions of poor farmers
> - heavy and prolonged rains in the monsoon season fill the rivers to bursting point
>
> - the Himalaya mountain range to the north increases precipitation intensity, and meltwater from snow in the mountains adds to river discharge
> - deforestation is widespread, and has increased with rapid population growth
> - flood management schemes such as dams and levees provide only limited protection from floods

North Devon/Cornwall (UK)

In the UK, several communities on the north coast of Devon and Cornwall experience high flood risks. Major flash floods occurred at Lynmouth in north Devon in 1953, and at Boscastle in north Cornwall in 2004. The causes of flooding in this area are:

- onshore winds bring warm moisture-laden air from the Atlantic Ocean which is uplifted as it meets the uplands of Exmoor and Bodmin Moor. This can trigger torrential downpours

- the steep drainage basins on the Lyn, Valency and other rivers, together with their impermeable geology and sparse tree cover, result in rapid runoff
- villages such as Lynmouth and Boscastle are vulnerable because they occupy the floors of steep, narrow valleys down which the floodwaters are funnelled

Impact of flooding

Revised ☐

Case study **Lower Severn floods, Gloucestershire and Worcestershire, 2007**

Causes The Lower Severn Valley in Gloucestershire and Worcestershire suffered severe flooding in July 2007. The floods followed an extreme rainfall event on 20 July, when 135 mm of rain fell at Pershore in Worcestershire in just 16 hours. Flash floods in several local tributary catchments raised the level of the Severn at Worcester nearly 6 m above normal. The severity of flooding was increased by heavy antecedent rainfall throughout the Severn basin: soils were already saturated by record rainfall in June.

Impact By 21 July there was widespread flooding all along the River Severn from Upton to Gloucester. Floods also hit towns and villages on the River Avon (a major tributary of the Severn). At Tewkesbury, floodwaters entered the town's ancient abbey for the first time in 247 years. Near Gloucester, floodwaters shut down an electricity substation, leaving 50,000 households without power for up to 2 days. A water treatment plant in Tewkesbury was also flooded, cutting water supplies to 140,000 households for 5 days. Some 10,000 motorists were left stranded on the M5 and surrounding roads and were forced to abandon their cars because of floodwater and landslides. The total insured losses were estimated at between £1 billion and £1.5 billion. There was also large-scale damage to property and disruption of businesses. Approximately 27,000 domestic insurance claims and 6,800 business claims were made. Crops were submerged and maize, potatoes and hay crops destroyed.

Case study **Pakistan floods, 2010**

Cause The floods of August and September 2010 were the worst to hit Pakistan for 80 years. Their main cause was extreme rainfall from the monsoon. At its peak, discharge on the River Indus was 40 times above normal and the floods covered one-fifth of the country.

Impact The human costs were high: a final death toll of approximately 2,000 with at least 1.2 million homes destroyed and whole villages swept away. Approximately 10 million people were displaced and 8 million needed emergency relief aid. Shortages of food and clean drinking water and inadequate sanitation were widespread. By September millions were at risk from water-borne diseases such as cholera and diarrhoea.

But humanitarian problems were dwarfed by the floods' economic costs, estimated between $3.5 billion and $5 billion. For 2010–11, Pakistan's GDP was forecast to fall by 2%. Massive damage was inflicted on the country's physical infrastructure (e.g. roads, bridges, power plants) and agriculture. Agriculture was worst affected: 3.2 million ha of crops were either lost or badly damaged. Commercial crops such as cotton and sugar cane were seriously affected, and there was a 20–30% decline in the output of food crops such as rice and wheat. The impact on agriculture was particularly significant because agriculture contributes one-fifth of Pakistan's GDP and employs 45% of the country's workforce. Poor farmers and landless labourers, with few resources to cope with disaster, were worst affected. Despite a major international relief effort, 2 months after the disaster there were still concerns of the possible spread of disease and malnutrition during the winter.

Examiner's tip

Exam answers to questions on flood hazards must differentiate clearly between the causes, effects and responses; assess (as well as describe) the impact of floods in human, environmental and economic terms; and evaluate risk in terms of society's exposure and vulnerability to flood hazards.

Flood management strategies

There are two contrasting flood management strategies:

- **hard engineering** — a structural approach involving the construction of dams, levees, spillways, etc.
- **soft engineering** — non-structural approaches, including flood forecasts, warnings, land use management

Hard engineering

Revised

Hard engineering strategies (Table 1.3) aim to confine floodwater to river channels or divert it to temporary storage in reservoirs and on floodplains by building structures such as dams and levees. These strategies are expensive to implement and often have undesirable environmental effects. However, some structures, such as dams, may offer benefits in addition to flood protection: multipurpose dams often provide water supplies, resources for recreation and leisure, and HEP.

Table 1.3 Structural approaches to flood protection

Scheme	Description
Embankments/levees	Embankments on either side of channels to increase channel capacity. Potentially hazardous if the water level is above the floodplain. Unless set back from the channel, levees raise water levels and increase flood risks.
Channel straightening/ channelisation	Removing meanders steepens the average gradient, increases the flow velocity and scours and deepens the channel. Eventually, meanders will re-form unless the new channel is lined with concrete.
Flood relief channels	Artificial channels that take some of the floodwater to relieve natural channels, e.g. Jubilee River on the Thames in Berkshire.
Sluice gates	Sluice gates are raised during times of flood to protect settlements downstream. Water is diverted into flood basins or washlands, where it is stored temporarily, e.g. River Wyre at Garstang in Lancashire.
Dam building	Storage of floodwaters in reservoirs or flood storage basins. Dams and reservoirs offer multipurpose usage, such as water supply, HEP, and recreation and leisure, as well as flood prevention (e.g. Kielder Water).
Channel enlargement	Increasing the width and depth of river channels through dredging to provide greater capacity. 'Clearing and snagging' are also used to remove vegetation and other debris from river channels, which increases channel cross-sectional area and flow velocity.

Soft engineering

Revised

Non-structural approaches to flood protection are increasingly favoured. They are cheaper, less environmentally damaging and more sustainable than hard engineering alternatives. The main non-structural approaches are summarised in Table 1.4.

> **Examiner's tip**
>
> Adopt a critical view of flood management strategies, showing understanding of environmental and economic pros and cons, as well as their sustainability.

Table 1.4 Non-structural approaches to flood protection

Scheme	Description
Floodplain management	Floodplains are attractive for settlement because they offer flat land that is easily developed and are locations for river crossings and transport routes. Pressure to develop floodplains in the UK is driven by population growth, societal changes and land shortages. However, floodplain development has significant flood risks, which will increase with climate change. Development also drains wetlands — natural storage areas for floodwater. Increasingly, planners in the UK guide new development away from floodplains, arguing that it is unsustainable. **River restoration** aims to restore rivers and their floodplains to their natural state — removing levees, re-coupling rivers with their floodplains, re-establishing meanders and wetlands, etc. Apart from its aesthetic and recreation value river restoration reduces the flood risk. Sustainable **river bank conservation** can be achieved by planting vegetation that binds bank material and absorbs flow energy. Planting 'live' willow stakes to stabilise banks is particularly effective.
Flood forecasts and flood warnings	In England and Wales, the Environment Agency operates a flood warning system. Flood warnings are issued by the agency through its telephone Floodline and its website. There are three levels of warning: flood alert, flood warning and severe flood warning. The system encourages people and organisations at risk to take action (e.g. evacuation) to mitigate the worst effects. Maps published online by the Environment Agency show the flood hazard areas and allow households to assess the general level of flood risk to their property.
Flood insurance	One mitigating option for people and organisations exposed to flood risk is flood insurance. In the UK, insurance companies are using GIS to provide more accurate estimates of the flood risk to individual properties. Typical flood insurance covers damage to property, loss of life, debris removal, relocation expenses and the cost of materials and equipment such as sandbags and pumps.
Flood abatement	Flood abatement aims to slow the movement of water into river channels. Its effect is to lengthen lag times and reduce peak discharge. This can be achieved through land use change and land use management in the upper catchment by afforestation, the conversion of arable to pasture, terracing, contour ploughing and reducing artificial land drainage. Flood abatement policies often experience problems where land is privately owned and it is difficult to get agreement on changes in land use and farming practices. Whole-catchment planning may also be hindered where administrative boundaries do not coincide with the watersheds of river basins. Flood abatement is a long-term strategy and may do little to reduce flooding in the short term.

Now test yourself

12 Make a list of the physical and human causes of river floods.

13 What is the difference between the exposure and vulnerability of a population to flood risks?

14 What factors influence (a) flash floods, (b) slow floods?

15 Give two examples of hard and soft engineering flood management strategies.

16 Give three advantages of soft engineering compared with hard engineering approaches to flood management.

Answers on p. 119

Check your understanding

1 Explain what Hjulström's curve tells us about river erosion, transport and deposition.

2 Compare the human, economic and environmental impacts of the Severn Valley flood (2007) and the Indus Valley flood (2010).

3 List the possible reasons why flood hazards often have a greater impact in LEDCs than in MEDCs.

4 Make notes in the form of a table of the human, environmental and economic advantages and disadvantages of (a) soft engineering and (b) hard engineering flood management strategies.

Answers on p. 119

Exam practice

1 (a) Outline the main processes of river erosion. [4]

 (b) Study Figure 1.3 which shows Hjulström's curve. Describe the relationship between velocity and load for the process of sediment deposition. [4]

 (c) Describe and explain the formation of floodplains. [7]

 (d) Describe and explain the main features of fluvial erosion associated with upland river valleys. [15]

2 (a) Describe the influence of vegetation and land use on river flow. [4]

 (b) Study Figure 1.2, which shows flow pathways in a drainage basin. Explain how water movement through different flowpaths can affect river discharge. [4]

 (c) Explain the importance of bankfull discharge for fluvial processes and the formation of channel landforms. [7]

 (d) Discuss the advantages and disadvantages of soft engineering for flood management strategies. [15]

Answers and quick quiz 1 online

Online

Examiner's summary

Explanation of river landforms requires a thorough understanding of physical processes.

✔ The relative importance of river erosion, transport and deposition varies in different parts of a river's course and over short distances. These changes are driven by variations in potential energy related to channel gradient, discharge, bank material etc.

✔ Rivers are energy systems. Knowledge of the relationships between river energy and erosion, transport and deposition is crucial to understanding fluvial processes and landforms.

✔ Explanations of the fluvial processes and the formation of fluvial landforms must convey their complexity, and the interaction of processes, sediments and geology over time.

✔ Increases in energy inputs to river systems result in rejuvenation and the creation of new landforms.

✔ Each drainage basin has unique physical characteristics that are reflected in its storm hydrograph.

✔ The interpretation of storm hydrographs and the ability to infer the fixed properties of drainage basins (e.g. geology, slopes, vegetation cover) and to assess the flood risks, are important skills.

✔ The impact of a river flood is determined by a society's exposure and vulnerability.

✔ People in LEDCs are more vulnerable to river floods than those in MEDCs; therefore flood hazards are more likely to become flood disasters in LEDCs.

✔ Human as well as physical factors are involved in the causes of river floods. Assessment of the relative importance of each to an actual flood event is needed.

✔ In response to questions on flood management strategies, evaluation of the strengths and weaknesses of hard and soft engineering approaches is often required. This should consider economic and environmental factors, together with their sustainability.

2 Cold environments

Distribution of cold environments

Cold climates that support glaciers, ice sheets and permafrost occur in high-latitude and high-altitude areas. The largest expanses of snow and ice are in polar regions, principally in the ice sheets of Antarctica and Greenland. Most of the world's highest mountain ranges — Himalayas, Andes, Alps and Rockies — also support icefields and glaciers. Periglacial environments occupy sub-Arctic Canada, Alaska and Siberia. In these regions glaciers and ice sheets are absent, but temperatures are so low that the ground is permanently frozen.

Glaciers as systems
Revised

The **glacial budget** (or mass balance) is the difference between a glacier's yearly accumulation and yearly ablation (melting, sublimation) of snow. There are three states of mass balance:

● positive — accumulation exceeds ablation, increasing the ice mass and causing the glacier to advance

● negative — ablation is greater than accumulation; the glacier shrinks and retreats upvalley

● neutral — accumulation and ablation are equal; the glacier's terminus remains static

The upper part of a glacier where ice accumulation exceeds ablation, is the **accumulation zone** (Figure 2.1). In the lower part, or **ablation zone**, ablation is greater than accumulation. The boundary between the accumulation zone and the ablation zone is the equilibrium or **firn line**. Above the firn line, the glacier surface is snow-covered.

The Nisqually Glacier on Mt Rainier in Washington State retreated steadily from 1840 to 1951. However, following high snow accumulation between 1944 and 1951, the glacier advanced to its present position, where it has remained more or less stationary for the last 20 years.

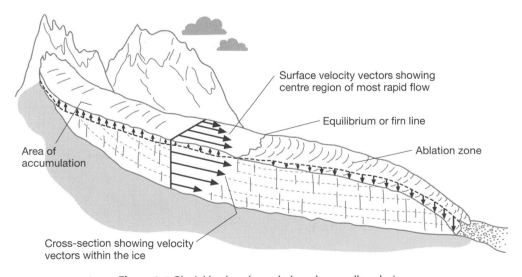

Figure 2.1 Glacial budget (mass balance) at a valley glacier

Ice movement

Revised

Glaciers move in two ways: by internal deformation and by sliding.

- In climates of extreme cold, glaciers are frozen permanently to the underlying bedrock, therefore these **cold-based glaciers** are incapable of much erosion. This explains how delicate landforms such as **tors** can survive glaciation. Cold-based glaciers move by **internal deformation** caused by the weight of ice and gravity: ice crystals in the glacier rearrange into parallel layers and slide past each other.

- In **warm-based glaciers**, 90% of movement occurs through **basal sliding**. A film of water at the base of the glacier lubricates the ice and facilitates sliding. Therefore, glaciers in temperate regions can move rapidly. Slope steepness and ice volume also influence rates of glacier flow. Fast-moving, warm-based glaciers are active agents of erosion. Glaciers occupying cirque hollows in the mountains exhibit a **rotational flow**. Driven by gravity and lubricated by basal meltwater the ice slides downslope. Viewed in cross-section, this movement is rotational.

Variations in the velocity of glacier movement give rise to **extensional flow** and **compressional flow**. Steep bedrock gradients accelerate ice flow and cause glaciers to thin. This is extensional flow. Where gradients are reduced and flow speeds slacken, glaciers increase in thickness and compressional flow dominates. Erosion is concentrated in areas between extensional and compressional flow where above-average flow velocities combine with relatively thick ice.

> **Typical mistake**
>
> Pressure, caused by the mass of ice and constrictions in glacier flow, causes ice to melt at temperatures well below freezing.

> **Now test yourself**
>
> 1 Define the terms: accumulation zone, ablation zone, equilibrium line.
> 2 Draw input–output diagrams to explain why glaciers (a) advance, (b) retreat.
> 3 What are warm- and cold-based glaciers and how effective are they as agents of erosion?
> 4 Name two ways in which glaciers move.
>
> **Answers on p. 120**

Glacial processes

Weathering

Revised

Freeze–thaw is the dominant weathering process in cold environments. When water freezes, its volume increases by 9%. If freezing occurs in confined spaces such as joints and rock crevices, the ice exerts enormous pressure on the surrounding rock. The forces involved are sufficient to break apart even the most resistant rocks. This is **frost wedging**.

The main influence on rates of frost wedging is the number of **freeze–thaw cycles**. Other influences are the availability of liquid water and rock type.

- Rocks disintegrate by freeze–thaw action more rapidly where plenty of liquid water is available. For this reason, dry tundra areas and cold deserts experience less freeze–thaw weathering than many temperate humid environments.

- Rocks vary in their susceptibility to freeze–thaw weathering. Tough gritstones and granites are more resistant than soft shales or porous chalk. The latter absorb water that, when it freezes, **shatters** the rocks into fragments. Well-jointed rocks (e.g. Carboniferous limestone) are also more susceptible to freeze–thaw weathering than massively jointed rocks (e.g. gritstone).

> **Typical mistake**
>
> The frequency of freeze–thaw cycles (i.e. the number of days when temperatures fluctuate above and below freezing) determines the effectiveness of freeze–thaw weathering, not uniform subzero temperatures.

Most **chemical weathering** processes are more effective in warm climates. However, **solution** of carbonate rocks such as chalk and limestone is an exception. Rates of solution increase at lower temperatures, making solution an important weathering process in cold environments.

Rainwater, containing carbon dioxide from the atmosphere and the soil, is a weak carbonic acid. It attacks and dissolves rocks such as limestone. This is the process of **carbonation**.

Erosion
Revised

Glaciers erode by **abrasion** and by **quarrying**.

- Rock particles frozen into a glacier and dragged along at the base of the glacier scour and abrade the bedrock. This process of abrasion rounds and smoothes rock outcrops. Fine-grained particles may polish the bedrock and coarser particles may leave deep scratches called **striations** (or striae).

- Quarrying (or plucking) removes bedrock particles along joints and bedding planes. For example, a small rock outcrop at the base of a glacier will cause frictional resistance to ice flow. On the upstream side, high pressure causes melting and the meltwater runs into joints and fissures in the rock. On the downstream side where pressure is lower, refreezing occurs. Thus as the glacier moves forward it quarries rock particles along joints in low pressure areas. The process of pressure melting and refreezing is known as **regelation**.

> **Examiner's tip**
>
> When explaining glacial features it is important to make clear the link between processes and landforms.

Glacial erosional landforms

Corries, arêtes, pyramidal peaks
Revised

Corries (also known as cirques) are deep, amphitheatre-like rock basins cut into mountainsides. Formed by glacial erosion, cirques in the northern hemisphere occur most frequently on north- and east-facing slopes.

Corrie glaciers develop on these slopes because of:
- the accumulation of blown snow from prevailing southwesterly winds
- the colder microclimate (e.g. longer periods of shadow)

A possible sequence of events leading to cirque formation involves:
- freeze–thaw beneath a snow patch (**nivation**) and the removal of debris by **surface wash** and **solifluction** to create a shallow depression
- snow turns to glacier ice and slides/flows downslope, overdeepening the depression by abrasion and quarrying
- the backwall of the overdeepened depression retreats by freeze–thaw weathering, while glacial erosion further deepens the depression (Figure 2.2)

In a fully developed cirque glacier, the weight of ice in the upper section of the glacier causes a rotational sliding movement that overdeepens the

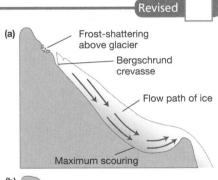

(a) Frost-shattering above glacier
Bergschrund crevasse
Flow path of ice
Maximum scouring

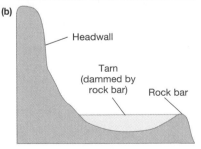

(b) Headwall
Tarn (dammed by rock bar)
Rock bar

Figure 2.2 Cross-section of a cirque glacier. (a) During the early stages of glaciation, the hollow becomes progressively overdeepened. (b) After glaciation, the overdeepened basin is occupied by a lake or tarn.

rock basin by abrasion. However, at the outlet of the basin, where ice movement is directed upwards, erosion is less severe and a rock bar or **lip** forms. A deep crevasse known as a **bergschrund** develops between the glacier and the headwall. Meltwater accumulates here and may assist quarrying on the headwall.

If two adjacent cirque glaciers cut back their headwalls and converge, they may reduce a broad ridge to a knife-edged feature called an **arête** (e.g. Crib Goch in Snowdonia). When three or more cirque glaciers converge in this way, they form a **pyramidal peak** (e.g. the Matterhorn).

Glacial troughs and associated features

Revised

Glacial troughs (or glacial valleys) are channel landforms, carved through solid rock by valley glaciers and **ice streams** (areas of more rapid flow within ice sheets). They probably developed along valleys that existed prior to glaciation. Glacial troughs are:

- roughly parabolic or U-shaped in cross-section — the result of glacial erosion of both the valley sides and the valley floor
- deeper than tributary valleys occupied by smaller glaciers. Because erosion rates of glaciers in major valleys are greater than those of smaller tributary glaciers, on deglaciation tributary valleys are left **hanging** above the main glacial trough
- straighter than river valleys, with projecting spurs planed off or **truncated**
- irregular in long profile. The upper part of the trough often has a steep rock wall known as a **trough head**. Further downvalley, rock basins are carved in areas of more intense erosion (e.g. where the valley narrows or tributary glaciers join the main glacier). Following deglaciation, these basins may form **ribbon lakes**

> **Examiner's tip**
>
> Glacial landforms are complex — the result of numerous glaciations of varying intensity over the past 1 million years or so. You must convey this complexity in your explanations of glacial landforms.

> **Typical mistake**
>
> Students often assume that glacial erosional landforms simply result from erosion by valley glaciers (alpine glaciation). In fact, many features formed when landscapes were buried beneath regional and continental ice sheets, such as those in Antarctica today.

Glacial depositional landforms

Glacial deposition

Revised

Glaciers are like huge conveyor belts for transporting rock debris. This rock debris derives from:

- glacial erosion of the valley sides and valley floor
- rockfall due to weathering of valley slopes
- rock avalanches and other mass movements from valley slopes

Eventually, this rock debris is deposited:

- at the ice front or terminus of the glacier
- under the glacier
- under the ice and beyond the ice front by meltwater flowing within and from the glacier

Collectively, these glacial deposits are called **glacial drift**. Large pieces of rock transported by ice, which are of different geology to the area where

Exam practice answers and quick quizzes at **www.therevisionbutton.co.uk/myrevisionnotes**

they are deposited, are known as **erratics** (e.g. Shap granite blocks from Cumbria found in Lancashire, Cheshire and Teesside).

Rock debris deposited in contact with glacier ice comprises an unsorted mix of particles of all sizes. This material is known as **till** or boulder clay. It may be transported on the surface (supraglacial), within (englacial) or beneath (subglacial) the ice. Some till is also bulldozed downvalley ahead of the glacier. **Moraine** is till that has been piled into a variety of hummocky mounds and ridges.

Lateral moraines

Lateral moraines form along the sides of valley glaciers. They consist of piles of loose, supraglacial rock debris derived from rockfall avalanching on to the glacier from the adjacent valley slopes. If the glacier recedes or shrinks, this debris forms prominent ridges that run parallel to the valley sides.

Terminal moraines

Moraine is delivered to the terminus or snout of a valley glacier by the forward movement of glacial ice. If the snout remains stationary for prolonged periods, the moraine accumulates to form a low ridge or **terminal moraine** across the valley. Retreating glaciers intermittently leave behind a succession of smaller **recessional moraines**.

Medial moraines

Where two glaciers meet, two adjacent lateral moraines merge to form a central **medial moraine** on the glacier surface.

Hummocky moraines

Hummocky moraines form chaotic landscapes, often made up of hundreds of steep-sided mounds (up to 50 m in height). They have no consistent orientation or linear development. These moraines are associated with dead or wasting ice.

Drumlins

Drumlins are smooth, oval-shaped hills made of till. They have a streamlined form, elongated in the direction of ice flow. Typical dimensions are 5–50 m in height and 1–2 km in length. In profile, drumlins have a short, steep slope (stoss) which faces up-glacier and a gentle long slope (tail) which faces down-glacier. Drumlins occur in swarms often in lowlands (e.g. Vale of Eden) close to centres of ice dispersal.

There are several theories of drumlin formation. The most widely accepted suggests that moraine beneath an ice sheet was eroded into streamlined forms by moving ice.

> **Examiner's tip**
>
> It is important to distinguish between extensive moraines such as glacial drift and drumlins deposited by ice sheets, and smaller-scale, localised moraines left by valley glaciers (e.g. lateral moraines, medial moraines).

Fluvio-glacial landforms

Fluvio-glacial deposits are laid down by meltwater streams and sorted by particle size into layers. Meltwater is an important agent of sediment transport and deposition in warm-based glaciers and during phases of deglaciation. Meltwater flows on the surface of glaciers, in tunnels within glaciers, at the base of glaciers, and beyond the ice front (proglacial). Landforms that result from fluvio-glacial deposition fall into two groups:

- proglacial features are deposited by meltwater streams beyond the ice front (e.g. sandur)
- ice-contact features are deposited by meltwater within glaciers (e.g. eskers, kames). These are shown in Figure 2.3

Outwash plains

Outwash plains (sandar) are extensive spreads of sand and gravel laid down by meltwater streams beyond the margin of glaciers and ice sheets. In southern Iceland, powerful meltwater streams draining several small icefields have deposited huge amounts of coarse sediment along the coast. As a result, the coastal plain has been extended several kilometres seaward. Proglacial lakes impounded between the ice front and recessional moraines also encourage rapid sedimentation by meltwater streams. Valley sandar develop in steep-sided glacial troughs that limit their lateral expansion.

Eskers

Eskers are sinuous ridges of sand and gravel that are often several kilometres long. They derive from sediments deposited within the channels of meltwater streams that flowed on, through or at the base of glaciers. Some eskers appear to run upslope — clear evidence that meltwater, under hydrostatic pressure, can flow uphill.

Kames and kame terraces

Cavities within glaciers such as crevasses may fill with sediment. Subsequent melting of the glacier causes the sediment to collapse to form an isolated mound or **kame**. Where sediments accumulate along ice margins (e.g. in a marginal lake between a glacier and the valley side), the eventual retreat of the ice leaves a continuous embankment parallel to the valley side. This is a **kame terrace**. The melting of ice cores trapped beneath glacial deposits may create surface depressions or **kettle holes** that later form small lakes.

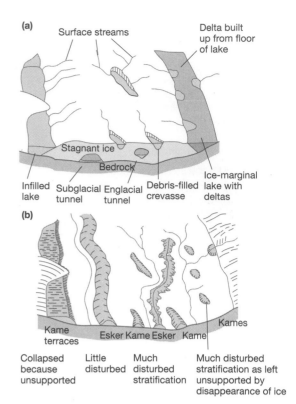

Figure 2.3 Fluvio-glacial features: (a) during glaciation and (b) after glaciation

Erosional landforms   Revised

Meltwater channels

Meltwater (or overflow) **channels** are the main glacio-fluvial erosional landform. These channels are subglacial in origin and were cut by meltwater streams with high discharge. Meltwater channels are usually steep-sided, deep and fairly straight. In long profile, some have up-gradients. This shows the influence of hydrostatic pressure, enabling water to flow uphill if there is sufficient force behind it. The high discharges needed to form large meltwater channels may be related to the formation of temporary lakes beneath glaciers. The North York Moors has several overflow channels cut by meltwater at the end of the last glacial period. The largest, Newtondale, is 15 km long, 80 m deep and was formed by

Typical mistake

Remember that fluvio-glacial deposits are distinguishable from ice-contact deposits (e.g. till) by the layering and sorting of sediment by size. In contrast, ice-contact deposits are unsorted mixtures of particles of all sizes (i.e. from boulders to clay).

meltwater draining proglacial Lake Eskdale. At its peak, discharge reached 10,000 cumecs.

Periglaciation

In high latitude and some high-altitude regions not covered by ice, temperatures are so low that the ground is permanently frozen. In this **periglacial** environment, geomorphological processes such as freeze–thaw and the growth of ice masses are dominant.

Today, the most extensive periglacial areas are in northern Canada and northern Siberia. However, periglacial areas were more widespread in the past. For example, southern Britain, although ice-free, experienced intensely cold periglacial conditions throughout the last glacial period.

Now test yourself

5 What is a freeze–thaw cycle? Why is freeze–thaw weathering most effective in environments with frequent freeze–thaw cycles?

6 Describe two glacial erosional processes.

7 List the typical landforms of alpine glaciation.

8 What is the difference between a valley glacier and an ice sheet?

9 What is the difference between moraines and fluvio-glacial deposits?

10 What is a drumlin; terminal moraine; esker; outwash plain?

Answers on p. 120

Periglacial processes   Revised

Permafrost

Permafrost is perennially frozen ground. Regions of continuous permafrost usually have a mean annual temperature of −5°C and below. Permafrost consists of two important layers: the **active zone** and the **frost zone**.

- The active zone lies near the surface and above the frost zone. It is here that freeze–thaw occurs. The frost melts during the summer before refreezing in the autumn.
- The frost table separates the active layer from the permanently frozen layer or frost zone. Unfrozen areas within the frost zone are known as **taliks**.

Ground ice

In periglacial areas, ice often exists as large segregated masses in the ground. When water freezes, its volume increases by 9%. If the ground has a high moisture content, the growth of ice crystals will attract remaining liquid water and lead to the development of segregated ice as lenses and veins. The result is local expansion (freezing) and contraction (melting) of the surface — a process that can produce a number of periglacial landforms.

Frost weathering and frost cracking

Frost weathering is an important process in periglacial environments. Numerous freeze–thaw cycles and the sparse cover of soil and vegetation mean that frost action is highly active. Subzero temperatures also cause the ground to crack by contraction. This process produces polygonal cracks similar to those formed in drying mud. Frost cracking is a major cause of patterned ground.

Frost heave

When water trapped in the **regolith** freezes its volume increases. As a result the ground surface is elevated, and the regolith moves slowly downslope under gravity. This is **frost heave**. Frost heave also involves

Typical mistake

The term 'permafrost' does not mean that the ground is permanently frozen. The top metre or so thaws in summer and this has an important influence on the periglacial environment.

the growth of columns of needle ice (just a few centimetres high) in the regolith, which push stones and finer particles towards the surface.

Nivation

Nivation is an erosive process that operates under and around snow patches. Meltwater percolates into rocks beneath the snow patch and causes intense freeze–thaw weathering. The resulting rock debris is then removed by surface wash and solifluction.

Solifluction

Solifluction is one of the most common processes in periglacial environments. It is defined as 'the slow flowing from higher to lower ground of masses of waste saturated with water'. Solifluction operates on slopes as gentle as 1–2° and on fine sand and silt. Movement is confined to the active layer. Rates of flow vary with climate, slope and vegetation cover, but are usually of the order of 1–10 cm per year.

Periglacial landforms
Revised

Patterned ground

Patterned ground, shown in Figure 2.4, is a characteristic feature of periglacial environments. It describes the distribution of rock particles in systems of polygons, nets, steps, stripes and circles.

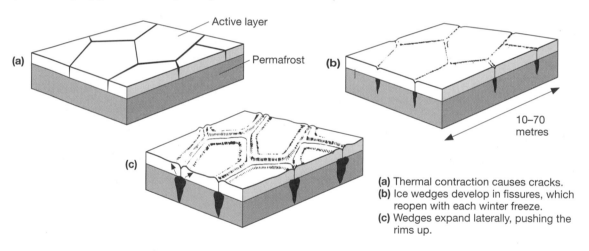

(a) Thermal contraction causes cracks.
(b) Ice wedges develop in fissures, which reopen with each winter freeze.
(c) Wedges expand laterally, pushing the rims up.

Figure 2.4 Patterned ground

Circles, nets and polygons normally occur on flat surfaces; steps and stripes form on slopes of between 5° and 30°. Frost cracking and frost heave are important processes in the development of patterned ground. Frost heave pushes larger stones to the surface and, because of the cambering of the surface, stones then move laterally. On steeply sloping ground, this cambering is oriented downslope. Coarser particles raised to the surface by frost heave roll into the depressions between the cambers. The result is alternating stripes of coarse and fine particles.

Ice wedges

Ice wedges are downward-tapering bodies of ice up to 10 m in depth. In plan they form a polygonal pattern at the surface. They appear to result from frost cracking. When an ice wedge melts, it may fill with sediment to form an **ice wedge cast**.

Pingos

The formation of ice lenses in the active layer can heave the overlying sediments into small symmetrical mounds (3–70 m high) known as **pingos**. Two theories describe the formation of pingos.

- Closed-system pingos develop beneath former lakes. Initially, the water in the lake prevents the surrounding regolith from freezing. Eventually, the lake fills with sediment. This reduces its insulating effect and the lake floor slowly freezes. As the permafrost advances, water trapped in sediments beneath the former lake is put under pressure, pushing the overlying sediments into a dome-shaped hill.
- Open system pingos originate when water trapped in a talik or in the active layer migrates under pressure through the frozen regolith. At a point of weakness, the water forces its way to the surface, forming a pingo.

Nivation hollows

Nivation creates shallow hollows or basins on upland surfaces. Once formed, **nivation hollows** are self-generating, trapping snow and promoting further freeze–thaw, surface wash and solifluction.

Solifluction lobes

Solifluction forms vast expanses of smooth terrain, often at angles as low as 1–3°. On steeper slopes, where solifluction flow is concentrated in well-defined linear paths, it often forms **solifluction lobes** where the gradient eases. Where flows are more uniform across slopes, terraces often develop. Some lobes and terraces are marked by large stones and boulders at their downslope ends, known as stone garlands or stone steps. Other lobes and terraces are turf-banked.

> **Examiner's tip**
>
> Some exam questions on periglaciation will invite you to describe and explain periglacial landforms. It is essential that you give equal weight to both command words. The most common error is to concentrate on description at the expense of explanation.
>
> The causes of some periglacial landforms are complex. Consider using sketches and annotated diagrams to assist explanation.

Exploitation and development in tundra areas

Tundra — a fragile environment
Revised

Cold environments support tundra ecosystems. **Arctic tundra** is found polewards of the boreal (coniferous) forest in Eurasia and North America. It is treeless, poorly drained and dominated by low relief. Much of this region is underlain by permafrost. Plant and animal species are adapted to low temperatures, prolonged snow cover, strong winds, short growing seasons and poor soils.

Arctic tundra is a fragile environment, vulnerable to climatic change and human activity. Any damage may be irreversible or reversible only over long periods. There are several reasons for this fragility:

- slow rates of soil formation and plant growth mean that **ecosystems** recover only slowly after change
- lack of **biodiversity** with simple **food webs** means that the decline of a single species can destabilise the ecosystem
- thawing of the permafrost is irreversible and triggers drastic geomorphological, hydrological and ecological change

Issue The Arctic National Wildlife Refuge (ANWR) is an important and fragile wilderness with protected status on Alaska's north slope. However, the US government wants to develop oil and gas reserves in the ANWR. The potential impact of development on the environment, ecosystems and indigenous people could be disastrous. The proposed development is in conflict with the conservation status of the ANWR.

Background and indigenous populations The ANWR is a wilderness area covering 80,000 km^2. The ecosystem is pristine and has remarkable biodiversity. There are 130,000 caribou and 45 mammal species including wolves, wolverines, musk oxen and polar bears. The ecosystem is highly productive during the brief arctic summer and attracts large numbers of migrant birds, fish and caribou. Indigenous populations such as the Inuit Inupiaq tribe and the Indian Gwich'in are traditional subsistence hunters and gatherers. Agriculture is impossible in such high latitudes. The Inupiaq live on the coast and rely on marine ecosystems. They hunt bowhead whales, polar bears, seals and walrus in the Beaufort Sea. They also hunt moose and salmon and gather berries. The Gwich'in depend for their survival on the Porcupine River caribou herd for food and raw materials. These traditional economies exist in balance with the arctic environment and have been sustainable for thousands of years.

Potential impact In 2005 the US Senate gave permission for exploratory drilling for oil and gas in Area 1002 in the ANWR. The decision was the culmination of a long battle between oil companies and conservationists. Permission was given for two main reasons:

- to achieve greater security of energy supplies
- to cut foreign energy imports and boost the USA's balance of payments

Both are in the national interest. However, conservationists argue that drilling will disrupt the calving and migration of the caribou, permanently harm the traditional way of life and culture of indigenous people, and damage the fragile tundra environment (oil spills, destruction of vegetation, melting of the permafrost). In addition, roads, pipelines and airstrips will have to be built on the tundra. Gravel will be extracted from stream and river beds for construction, adversely affecting freshwater ecosystems.

Management and sustainability The US government and oil companies say that modern technologies make oil and gas extraction less environmentally intrusive. Oil and gas reserves can be identified using controlled explosions, limiting the need for drilling and building access roads. Roads will be insulated from the permafrost on 'ice pads' and new drilling techniques allow oil and gas to be extracted several kilometres away from drilling rigs.

Background Antarctica, the fifth largest continent, is a cold desert. 99% of the continent is covered by ice, which is up to 5 km thick. In Antarctica the current ice age has lasted for 12 million years. Isolated and with an extreme climate, Antarctica has no permanent settlement. The continent is protected against development by international law — the Antarctic Treaty (AT) (1959).

Environmental issues Despite its protected status, Antarctica and the surrounding ocean face a number of environmental threats. These threats relate to its increasing accessibility and its resource potential. Tourism is growing rapidly. In 2007–08, 46,000 tourists visited Antarctica, three-quarters by cruise ship mainly to the Antarctic Peninsula. Tourism creates pollution and disrupts wildlife. Although tourist numbers are relatively small there are no sewage treatment facilities and in such a cold climate organic decomposition is very slow. Overfishing (often illegal and unregulated) is a further problem, severely depleting fish stocks (e.g. Patagonian toothfish). Krill (a type of shrimp) has been overfished. Krill are at the base of the marine food web and so overfishing of krill threatens

species higher up the food chain such as whales, seals and penguins. Fishing is also responsible for killing thousands of seabirds that become entangled in discarded fishing gear. Threats also come from potential oil spills and wastes from shipping and from offshore oil drilling.

Environmental protection and sustainability The AT designates Antarctica as 'a natural reserve, devoted to peace and science'.

Activities are regulated and their environmental impact assessed, e.g. protection of fauna and flora and waste management, in order to achieve sustainable use.

All activities relating to Antarctic mineral resources, except for scientific research, are forbidden.

Environmental Protocols since the AT was signed have further strengthened protection, prohibiting the introduction of non-native species and according some species special protection status.

Wastes must be reduced to a minimum; hazardous substances such as PCBs are banned and others are subject to stringent storage regulations.

More than 20 million km² of the Southern Ocean are covered by the AT. In these waters discharges of oil, noxious liquid substances and garbage are prohibited. There are also rules preventing the discharge of raw sewage and for emergency preparedness and response to potential environmental hazards.

Fish stocks in the Southern Ocean are managed by the Commission for the Conservation of Antarctic Marine Living Resources. The aim is to achieve a sustainable fishery. However, enforcing the conservation measures in a vast area of ocean is difficult.

Now test yourself

11 What is the difference between a glacial and a periglacial environment?

12 Define the terms: permafrost, active layer, talik.

13 What is a pingo?

14 How does solifluction affect the landscape of the tundra?

15 In what ways is the tundra a fragile environment?

Answers on p. 120

Check your understanding

1 Explain how fluctuations in the glacial budget can cause glaciers to advance and retreat.

2 Summarise in a table the main landforms of cold glacial environments. Classify the landforms according to (a) origin (glacial, fluvio-glacial, weathering) and (b) type (erosional/depositional).

3 Outline the problems caused by resource exploitation in a cold environment and how these problems can be minimised.

4 Describe how indigenous populations in cold environments have exploited local resources sustainably.

5 What are the development pressures in Antarctica and how are they being addressed?

Answers on p. 120

Exam practice

1 (a) Study Figure 2.1 which shows the mass balance (or glacier budget) of a valley glacier. Describe how glaciers function as systems. [4]

(b) Describe the types of flow associated with glacier movement. [4]

(c) Describe the main characteristics of lateral and terminal moraines and suggest reasons for their formation. [7]

(d) To what extent do you agree that economic development in tundra areas and/or the Southern Ocean is, in the long term, unsustainable? [15]

2 (a) Describe the global distribution of periglacial environments. [4]

(b) Describe and explain how permafrost influences landscape in periglacial environments. [4]

(c) Study Figure 2.4 which shows patterned ground, a characteristic landform of periglacial environments. Describe and explain the formation of patterned ground. [7]

(d) Why are cold environments fragile and how can they be managed sustainably? [15]

Answers and quick quiz 2 online

Online

Examiner's summary

✔ To explain a glacier's annual budget and its response (i.e. advance, recession, stasis) you must understand the mass balance of inputs and outputs of snow, ice and water.

✔ Glacier movement takes place through flows and slides. These movements may be rotational, compressional and extensional. It is important to know how erosion occurs at the base of a glacier and the erosional effects of rotation, compression and extension.

✔ Classic erosional features such as corries, arêtes and pyramidal peaks are associated with valley glaciers and alpine glaciation.

✔ Emphasise the relationship between processes and form in explanations of glacial (and other) landforms.

✔ Explanations of glacial landforms must convey their complexity — how they reflect different intensities of glaciation over the past 2 million years.

✔ Glacial deposits comprise those laid down directly by ice (i.e. moraines) and those deposited by meltwater (fluvio-glacial). Unlike moraines, fluvio-glacial features may be formed at considerable distances in advance of the ice front.

✔ It is important to appreciate the differences between glacial deposits associated with valley glaciers (e.g. valley moraines) and those left by continental ice sheets (e.g. drumlins, till plains).

✔ The keys to understanding periglacial landforms are permafrost and ground ice. The resulting landforms are less spectacular than those of glaciated environments, but more widespread.

✔ Questions inviting descriptions and explanations of landforms must achieve a good balance — too often description is emphasised at the expense of explanation.

✔ Indigenous groups have lived sustainably in cold environments for thousands of years. Today, the environment and the traditional ways of life of these groups are increasingly threatened by economic development and the exploration and extraction of minerals and energy resources.

✔ Consider using sketches and diagrams to assist explanations of physical landforms.

✔ There is often conflict in cold environments between development and conservation. Strategies for conservation and sustainable development in places such as Alaska and Antarctica should be evaluated.

3 Coastal environments

The coastal system

The coast is an **open system**. Inputs of energy from waves, winds and tides interact with geology, sediments, plants and human activities to produce distinctive coastal landforms. The coast is a dynamic place where change (rockfall, landslides, etc.) often occurs rapidly. This suggests that some parts of the coastal system have yet to achieve a steady state. Given that today's coastline is only 6,000 years old (i.e. the rise in sea level that followed the last glacial ended 6,000 years ago), this is not surprising.

> An **open system** has inputs, outputs and throughputs of both energy and materials.

Energy inputs Revised ☐

Waves

Waves are superficial undulations of the water surface caused by winds blowing across the sea surface. They are the main source of energy that drives the coastal system. Waves consist of orbital movements of water molecules that diminish with depth. In fact, water in a wave moves forward only when it approaches the shore and breaks. Wave power is proportional to the square of a wave's height and its velocity.

Wave power is influenced by the openness of a coastline, the depth of water in the nearshore zone, the wind's strength and duration, and the length of open ocean over which the wave has been generated (**fetch**).

On the basis of their energy characteristics, waves can be divided into **constructive** and **destructive** types. Constructive waves transport sand and **shingle** onshore and build beaches. Typically they are less than 1 m high, have short **wave lengths** and low energy. Destructive waves erode beach material and transport it offshore. These waves are steeper, with longer wave lengths, powerful **backwash** and high energy.

> **Wave length** is the horizontal distance between wave crests.
>
> **Backwash** describes the seaward movement of water down a beach under the influence of gravity.

Tides

Tides are caused by the gravitational pull of the Moon and Sun on the oceans. Twice a month, when the Moon, Sun and Earth are aligned, the tidal force is strongest. This situation produces a **spring tide** and the highest monthly tidal ranges. The lowest tidal ranges — **neap tides** — also occur twice a month when the Sun and Moon in relation to Earth are positioned at right angles to each other.

Tides are an important source of energy in the coastal system. They generate powerful currents that transport huge amounts of water and fine sediment. The average tidal range also influences coastal landforms. Features such as mudflats and salt marshes dominate lowland coasts with high tidal ranges (over 4 m). In contrast, on coastlines with narrow tidal ranges (e.g. 2 m or less), wave action dominates, favouring the formation of beaches, offshore bars and barrier islands.

> **Typical mistake**
>
> It is a mistake to assume that destructive waves create erosional features and constructive waves depositional features. The nomenclature refers to the ability of waves to transport sediment in the coastal zone. Constructive waves tend to deposit sediment along the shoreline and build beaches. Destructive waves erode beaches, removing sediment which is then deposited offshore.

Sediment sources

The sediments that form beaches, mudflats and other depositional features originate from three sources: cliff erosion, offshore areas and rivers.

- Cliff erosion provides only a small fraction of beach sediments (around 5%).

- Some sediments have been combed from the shallow sea bed offshore. As a result of deglaciation, sea level has risen by around 100 m in the last 18,000 years. During this time, alluvium originally deposited by rivers on exposed continental shelf areas has been gradually swept shorewards by rising seas and wave action.

- Rivers are the main source of coastal sediments (around 90%). Sand and shingle are transported into the coastal system through river mouths as bedload; silt and clay as suspended load.

> **Examiner's tip**
>
> Don't overlook the importance of tides and winds in the formation of coastal features. Some coastlines are dominated by tidal processes (e.g. estuaries); others by wind action (e.g. dunes).

Sediment cells

Coastal sediments are confined to well-defined stretches of coastline known as **sediment cells**, with little movement of sediment between adjacent cells (Figure 3.1). Sediment cells, defined by prominent physical features such as headlands and estuaries, provide the geographic framework for coastal management in the UK.

> **Typical mistake**
>
> It is a common misconception to think that coastal sediments are mainly derived from cliff erosion. Rivers and the offshore zone are more important.

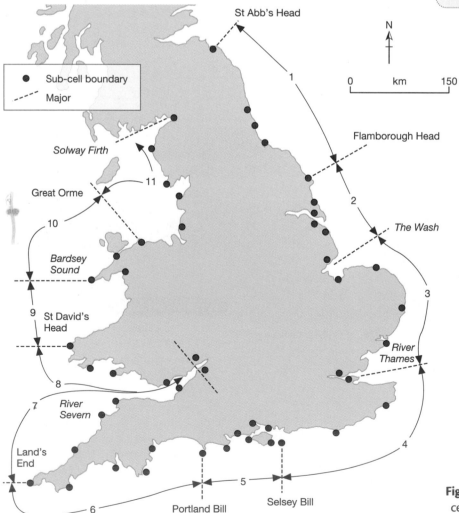

Figure 3.1 Coastal sediment cells in England and Wales

Exam practice answers and quick quizzes at **www.therevisionbutton.co.uk/myrevisionnotes**

Coastal processes

Marine erosional processes

Revised

Wave action on coasts induces three erosional processes: **abrasion** (or corrasion), **hydraulic action** (or quarrying) and **corrosion** (Table 3.1). These processes are most important when high-energy waves, associated with storm conditions, strike coastlines made of weak and incoherent rock.

Table 3.1 Marine erosion processes

Type of erosion	Process
Abrasion (corrasion)	High-energy waves pick up shingle and scour (abrade) the base of cliffs. The result is a wave-cut notch. The cliff is undermined and retreats through rockfall.
Hydraulic action (quarrying)	Air and water, forced under pressure into joints and bedding planes by storm waves, weaken rocks and cause collapse. The effectiveness of hydraulic action depends on the density of joints etc. in the rock. Hydraulic action also includes the impact of masses of water (wave shock or wave hammer), which loosens and dislodges rock particles.
Corrosion	Some rock minerals are susceptible to solution. For example, calcareous cements that bind sandstone particles may be attacked by solution, leading to rock disintegration.

Transportation and deposition

Revised

Wave action generates coastal currents which transport sediments (a) at right angles and (b) parallel to the shore. The former, which move sediment up and down beaches are known as **shore-normal currents**, the latter, responsible for sediment movement along beaches and parallel to the shore, are **longshore currents** (Figure 3.2).

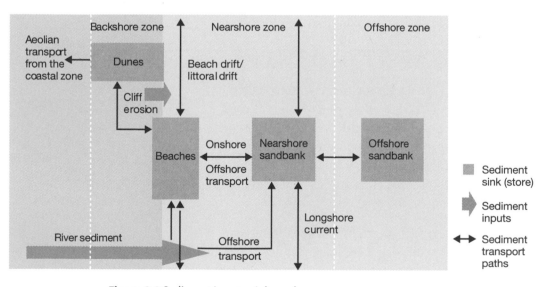

Figure 3.2 Sediment inputs, sinks and transport

Rip currents develop at right angles to the shore and form when there are marked differences in wave height in the nearshore zone. They transport sediments offshore and deposit them to form offshore bars.

Longshore drift is a process that transports sand and shingle laterally along beaches. As waves approach the shore obliquely, the **swash** runs up the beach at the same oblique angle. The backwash, however, is pulled down the beach by gravity at right angles to the shore. The result is a zig-zag pattern

> As waves break, water moves forward up and across the beach. This movement is known as **swash**.

of swash and backwash that transports sediment in the direction of the dominant waves. Meanwhile a longshore current moves suspended sand in the surf zone parallel to the shore. Longshore processes deposit sediments in the shore zone and form features such as spits and barrier beaches.

Subaerial processes   Revised ☐

Subaerial processes such as weathering and **mass movement** exert a strong influence on coastal scenery. This is particularly evident in weak rocks such as clay and shale, which are susceptible to rockfalls, slides, flows, surface runoff (e.g. surface wash) and gullying. Mass movements are triggered by:

- wave action undermining the base of cliffs
- heavy rainfall, which 'loads' slopes and weakens rocks such as clay
- steep coastal slopes (e.g. cliffs)

Weathering processes in coastal environments include wetting and drying as a result of waves, spray and tides; salt weathering; and solution weathering. Honeycomb rock surfaces in the spray zone are evidence of salt weathering. Rocks on the shoreline are also destroyed by biological weathering caused by organisms such as molluscs, sponges and sea urchins.

Landforms of erosion

Upland coastlines comprising resistant rocks support a range of erosional landforms. These features, which include cliffs and wave-cut platforms, headlands and bays, blow holes, arches and stacks, are the result of wave attack and the retreat of cliffs inland.

Cliffs   Revised ☐

On upland coasts the land often meets the sea abruptly to form steep **cliffs**. Despite erosion and subaerial processes, cliffs retain their steep profiles as they retreat inland because wave action continually removes debris produced by rockfall and mass movement. Rates of cliff recession are affected by the **structure** and **lithology** of cliffs, such as jointing, faulting and chemical composition. Abrasion may hollow out less resistant rocks; and mechanical erosion such as quarrying and wave hammer may result in collapse along major joints (see Table 3.1).

Lithology and structure are the dominant controls of **cliff profiles**. Resistant rocks, such as basalt and limestone, erode slowly and are stable at steep angles. In contrast, less resistant rocks, such as clay and shale, erode quickly and often form lower-angled profiles.

The angle of dip of sedimentary rocks is a major influence on cliff profiles.

- Horizontally bedded rocks, such as the chalk at Flamborough Head in Yorkshire and at Bat's Head in Dorset, form vertical cliffs. These cliffs, undermined by wave action, retreat parallel to themselves, maintaining their steep profiles by rockfall.
- Landward-dipping strata also form steep cliffs. This is because eroded and weathered rock particles are not easily dislodged from the cliff face.

> **Structure** refers to the physical characteristics of rocks, such as joints, faults and bedding.
> **Lithology** refers to the chemical composition of rocks.

- Seaward-dipping strata develop profiles that mirror the angle of dip of the **bedding planes**. Blocks weakened by erosion and weathering fail along these planes and slide into the sea.

Caves

Caves develop below the mean high water mark along lines of weakness such as joints, bedding planes and faults. Hydraulic action and abrasion loosen blocks along joints to create hollows that can be further exploited by waves.

Arches

Caves that form on opposite sides of headlands (where wave energy is highest) or along a narrow fin of rock that projects seawards, may form natural **arches** such as Durdle Door and the Green Bridge of Wales.

Stacks

The combination of marine and subaerial processes eventually leads to arch collapse (as at Marsden in Tyne and Wear in 1996), leaving isolated rock pinnacles or **stacks** (e.g. the Needles on the Isle of Wight).

Blow holes

If part of the roof of a tunnel-like cave running at right angles to the cliff line collapses along a master joint, it may form a vertical shaft that reaches the cliff top. This is a **blow hole**. If the entire roof of such a cave collapses, it creates a narrow inlet or **geo**. A natural arch may also develop if part of the cave roof remains intact at the seaward end of a geo (e.g. at Flamborough).

Wave-cut platforms

The final stage of cliff recession results in the ultimate erosional feature: a wide **wave-cut** or shore **platform**. This, the former base of the cliffs, is abraded by wave action and weathered by biological and chemical processes. The long profile of wave-cut platforms is controlled by the tidal range. Coastlines with a low tidal range (less than 4 m) have gently sloping platforms interrupted by a ramp at the high-tide mark and a small cliff at the low-tide mark. Erosion is concentrated at these two locations during the tidal cycle. On coastlines with a large tidal range, erosion is spread over a wider area of the platform. This creates a more uniform and steeper sloping platform.

> **Examiner's tip**
>
> Think of features such as caves, arches, stacks, blow holes and wave-cut platforms as temporary landforms that result from the retreat and degradation of cliffs.

> **Examiner's tip**
>
> Not all cliffed coastlines develop the classic suite of erosional landforms (e.g. caves, arches, stacks). Although less resistant rocks such as clay often form steep cliffs, they are lithologically too weak to support features such as caves, arches etc.

Headlands and bays

Revised

Headlands and bays are large-scale coastal features which often reflect differences in rock structure and lithology. **Headlands** are areas of more resistant rock that project seawards. **Bays**, situated adjacent to headlands, are large coastal indentations comprising less resistant rock. Headlands and bays form **discordant coastlines** where rocks of different hardness crop out at right angles to the coastline. This is the case at east Purbeck in Dorset where resistant chalk and limestone form the headlands of Ballard Point and Durleston Head, and areas of less resistant sands, gravels and clays are occupied by bays such as Studland and Swanage.

Headlands and bays can also develop along coastlines of uniform geology, but where there are variations in the degree of jointing and faulting. Along the chalk coastline of Flamborough in east Yorkshire, the more heavily faulted areas have been eroded into bays (e.g. Selwicks Bay) by wave action.

> **Now test yourself**
>
> 1 Name three sources of energy input to the coastal system.
>
> 2 What are the three main coastal erosional processes?
>
> 3 Explain briefly how each erosional process contributes to cliff recession.
>
> 4 Draw a diagram with labels to show the sequence of erosional landforms (from cliffs to wave-cut platforms) that develop through cliff recession.
>
> Answers on p. 121

Wave energy is high around headlands because of **wave refraction**. This explains the dominance of erosional landforms and the absence of beaches on headlands. In contrast, wave energy is low in bays, therefore deposition is widespread and beaches are well developed.

> **Wave refraction** describes the behaviour of waves, which in shallow water in the nearshore zone, bend and break parallel to the shoreline.

Beaches

Beaches are accumulations of sand and shingle in the shore zone. Two aspects of beach form are of particular interest: **beach profiles** and **beach plans**.

Beach profiles   Revised ☐

The cross-section of a beach between the mean high water mark and the mean low water mark is known as the beach profile. Beach profiles are determined by sediment size and wave type.

Shingle beaches are steeper and narrower than sand beaches. This is because shingle, being coarser than sand, has a higher **percolation rate**. As swash from a breaking wave pushes shingle up the beach, percolation results in a rapid loss of power. As a result there is little or no backwash to drag the shingle seawards. Thus the shingle is moved only in one direction. The outcome is a beach with a relatively steep angle (e.g. about 10°). Sand beaches, with lower percolation rates, have a longer swash and more powerful backwash. The outcome is a beach with a lower average slope angle.

The second influence on beach profiles is wave type. High-energy breakers produce wide, flat beaches. These waves have a powerful backwash and erode sand and shingle. The sediments are transferred offshore, where they form a **longshore bar**. Low-energy waves, in contrast, induce a net onshore transfer of sediments and beaches become steep, with prominent **beach faces** and ridges.

Beach plans   Revised ☐

In planform, beaches are either **swash-aligned** or **drift-aligned**. This distinction is based on their origins and predominant wave patterns.

Swash-aligned beaches

Swash-aligned beaches are uniform in plan, more or less straight and occur where waves are fully refracted (i.e. swash and backwash move along the same path, perpendicular to the shoreline). **Bay head beaches** are classic swash-aligned features. So, too, are many **barrier beaches** (e.g. Slapton Sands in south Devon), **tombolos** (e.g. Chesil Beach in Dorset) and offshore bars.

Drift-aligned beaches

Drift-aligned beaches such as **spits** and **barrier beach islands** develop on open coastlines. Here, waves are rarely fully refracted and sediment transport is dominated by longshore drift (Figure 3.3). Spits often form across estuaries (e.g. Spurn Head, east Yorkshire; Orford Ness, Suffolk) or where there is an abrupt change of direction in the coastline (e.g. Hurst Castle, Hampshire). Evidence of growth by longshore drift is shown by the **recurved** shingle ridges or laterals

> **Barrier beaches** are long, narrow beaches that form across bays and inlets. On their landward side they impound freshwater or brackish lagoons.
>
> **Tombolos** are beaches that join the mainland to an island.

of spits. These mark the former distal ends of spits and show the direction of growth. The distribution of spits around the UK appears to correlate with coastlines that have a low tidal range (less than 2 m). A low tidal range concentrates wave action in a narrow vertical band of coast.

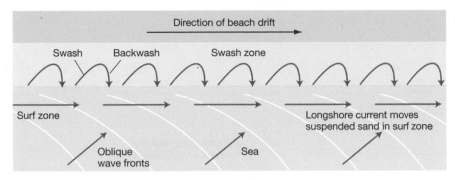

Figure 3.3 Longshore drift

Examiner's tip

Many beach types are classified according to their shape or planform rather than their formation (i.e. swash- or drift-aligned). This means that features such as spits, tombolos and barrier beaches could be either swash- or drift-aligned.

Beach berms, runnels and cusps
Revised

Beach berms, runnels and cusps are small-scale, temporary beach features. **Berms** are flat-topped ridges at the back of beaches which mark the upper limit of the swash zone during the previous tidal cycle.

Runnels are shallow beach depressions that run parallel to the shore. Separated by low ridges and often filled with water at low tide, they form as the tide migrates across the swash zone.

Beach **cusps** are crescent-shaped features spaced regularly along beaches. They vary in diameter from a few metres to 60 m and best develop on beaches where there is a mix of coarse and fine particles. Coarser particles accumulate on the horns of the cusp; finer particles occupy the embayments. Their formation, though not fully understood, is related to the division of the swash and a resulting cellular circulation. Once established, beach cusps are self-sustaining.

Dunes

Formation of dunes
Revised

Dunes are the only significant coastal landforms produced by the wind. The wind induces the movement of sand by the collision of particles. Larger particles move by **creep** on the surface of dunes, smaller particles are transported by a skipping process that extends up to 1 m or so above the surface. This is **saltation**.

Blown sand accumulates around objects such as logs and bottles. However, once these are buried, sand accumulation ends. Mature dunes only form when vegetation provides an obstacle to blown sand. This is because some plants, such as **marram** grass, thrive when submerged by sand. Burial stimulates growth, which in turn encourages further deposition. Deposition also occurs because plants reduce wind speeds near the ground surface. Thus by anchoring the sand, vegetation plays a key role in dune formation.

Sand dunes develop on lowland coastlines where there is:

- a plentiful supply of sand (possibly from nearby river estuaries)
- a shallow offshore zone, allowing extensive areas of sand to dry out at low tide
- an extensive backshore area where sand can accumulate
- prevailing onshore winds

Dune morphology

Revised

Coastal dunes form a series of **ridges** parallel to the coastline, as shown in Figure 3.4. The ridges decrease in height inland as sand supply diminishes. Depressions or **slacks** that reach down to the water table, separate the dune ridges. Coastal dunes usually have a steep windward slope and a less steep leeward slope. Sand eroded from the exposed windward slope is deposited on the sheltered leeward side. The older (or grey) dunes are immobile, stabilised by their vegetation cover. Where supplies of fresh sand are plentiful, dune systems extend seawards. This process is known as **progradation**.

Examiner's tip

One consequence of dunes stabilising inland, and new dunes forming near the shoreline, is that during periods of static sea levels, dune belts will extend seawards. However, contemporary rising sea level is resulting in the erosion of many dune systems.

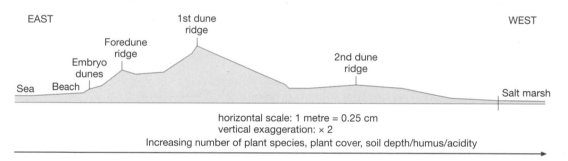

horizontal scale: 1 metre = 0.25 cm
vertical exaggeration: × 2
Increasing number of plant species, plant cover, soil depth/humus/acidity

Figure 3.4 Cross-section through the dunes at Alnmouth

Sand dunes are fragile environments. Destruction of the vegetation cover by grazing (e.g. rabbits) or human activities (e.g. trampling, firing) can lead to massive wind erosion and the formation of **blow-outs**. Frontal erosion of dunes by waves also occurs in storm conditions. Rising sea levels due to global warming are an increasing threat to coastal dune environments in the twenty-first century.

Now test yourself

5 What is a sediment cell?
6 Explain the processes that cause swash-alignment and drift-alignment of beaches.
7 Describe the formation of one type of drift-aligned beach.
8 Why are shingle (pebble) beaches generally (a) steeper, (b) narrower than sand beaches?
9 How does vegetation influence the formation of coastal dunes?
10 What is (a) a dune slack, (b) a blow-out?

Answers on p. 121

Salt marshes

Formation of salt marshes

Revised

Mudflats and **salt marshes** are landforms of sheltered, low-energy coastlines where wave action is weak. In quiet areas, such as estuaries and on the landward side of spits, tidal currents deposit fine sediment in suspension. Accretion leads to the growth of mudflats and salt marshes. Mudflats and salt marshes are associated with large tidal ranges which generate powerful currents that can transport large quantities of fine sediment.

Figure 3.5 is a cross-section through a salt marsh in the Aln estuary in Northumberland and shows a number of typical features:

- a low cliff, about half a metre high, separating the mudflats from the low marsh. Tidal scour maintains this cliff
- an abrupt break of slope dividing the high marsh from the low marsh
- a dense network of creeks and tributaries draining the marsh and bringing water in on the flood tide
- small salt pans located sporadically on the surface of the high marsh

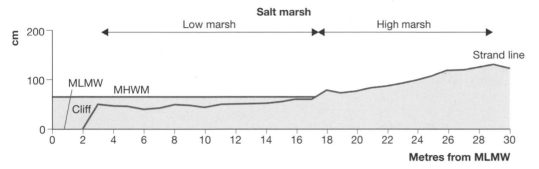

Figure 3.5 Cross-section through a salt marsh at Alnmouth, Northumberland

Vegetation plays a key role in the development of salt marshes. Many marshes show a zonation of species that is closely related to height above sea level, as shown in Table 3.2.

Table 3.2 Plant zonation on salt marshes

Environment	Environmental conditions	Plants
Mudflats	High salinity levels; low oxygen levels in mud; high turbidity; long periods of inundation on each tidal cycle.	No plants, only algae.
Low marsh	Less hostile conditions than mudflats, but salinity and turbidity still high and oxygen levels low. Tidal inundation shorter.	*Spartina* (cord grass) and *Salicornia* (glasswort) are the two common pioneer species. Sea blite (*Suaeda maritima*) and sea purslane (*Halimione portulacoides*) are found on better-drained areas (e.g. edges of creeks).
High marsh	Flooding only occurs on spring tides. Salinity levels are relatively low and soil develops.	Wide variety of species, including salt marsh grass (*Puccinellia*), sea rush (*Juncus maritimus*), sea lavender (*Limonium*), sea aster (*Aster tripolium*), sea blite (*Suaeda maritima*) and sea purslane (*Halimione portulacoides*).

Ecological succession drives the development of salt marshes and follows a number of stages.

- Colonisation by pioneer species such as cord grass and glasswort. These plants slow the movement of water and encourage rapid sedimentation (1–2 cm a year). Their roots help to stabilise the mud.
- Through accretion of sediment the marsh increases in height and conditions become more favourable for the invasion of other, less-tolerant species. Biodiversity and plant cover increase. Plants such as sea rush, sea aster, sea lavender, salt marsh grass and common scurvy grass dominate.
- The marsh height stabilises 1 m or so above the mean high-tide mark. With only occasional inundation on the highest spring tides, vertical accretion ends. Salinity levels drop and soil starts to develop.

At Happisburgh in northeast Norfolk coastal erosion rates often exceed 5 m a year. This rapid erosion has both physical and human causes. The coastline, comprising weak sands and gravels and soft clay, is easily undercut by wave action. Moreover, the long fetch to the north and northeast means that wave energy is high along this coast. However, erosion has accelerated considerably since 1990 when 300 m of the sea defences that protected Happisburgh (revetments) were destroyed by a storm. The decision not to repair the revetments increased erosion and led to the loss of six cliff-top homes. Under the current government policy of 'no active intervention' the village of Happisburgh could disappear before the end of the century.

Sea level change

Causes of sea level change
Revised

Absolute sea level change results from a worldwide rise or fall in the volume of water in the oceans. This is a **eustatic** change. During the last glacial, sea level was 100–120 m lower than today and large areas of the continental shelf around the British Isles were dry land.

Rising sea level, which causes the coastline to retreat, is called a **transgression**. This happens during interglacial periods, when ice sheets and glaciers melt. The opposite, **regression**, produces an advancing coastline. This occurs during glacials when huge volumes of water are frozen in ice sheets and glaciers. For example, in the last glacial, ice sheets and glaciers in the northern hemisphere occupied an area three times greater than today.

At a local scale, sea level change occurs if the land rises or sinks relative to sea level. This type of sea level change is associated with either **isostatic** or tectonic movements. Table 3.3 summarises sea level changes and their effects on coastal landforms.

> **Isostatic** change results from the loading and unloading of ice on the continents. During an ice age continental crust is 'loaded' and sinks by several hundred metres. When the ice melts, unloading occurs and the crust slowly rises by a similar amount. The result is a localised, relative change in sea level.

Table 3.3 Changing sea levels and coastal landforms in the British Isles

Glacio-eustacy	
Rising sea level (absolute — submergence)	
Shingle beaches (spits, bars, etc.)	River sediments deposited on the dry continental shelf during the last glacial when the shelf area was above sea level. Rising sea level in the last 20,000 years swept up the sediment and deposited it on present-day coasts.
Estuaries	Drowned, shallow lowland river valleys, e.g. Severn, Thames and Humber estuaries. Transgression flooded low-lying areas around the Wash and Somerset Levels.
Rias	Drowned, incised river valleys on upland coasts, e.g. southwest Ireland, River Dart (Devon), River Fal (Cornwall).
Fjords	Drowned glacial troughs.
Ancient shore platforms	Cut by wave action in the last interglacial when sea level was 8–10 m higher than today, e.g. at Start Bay in south Devon.
Glacio-isostacy	
Falling sea levels (relative — emergence)	
Raised beaches and relict cliffs	Ancient beaches and cliff lines elevated above sea level following deglaciation and the unloading of ice sheets from northern Britain, e.g. Applecross Peninsula, northwest Scotland (8 m above sea level).
Tectonic movements	
Earthquakes/faulting	Localised tectonic movements leading to submergence or emergence, e.g. Alaskan earthquake in 1964 raised part of the Alaskan coast by 4–9 m.

Impact of sea level change

Revised

Sea level change has consequences for both the physical and the human environment.

Physical impact

- More extensive erosion on cliffed coastlines because waves attack areas previously above the highest tides.

- The erosion of more fragile landforms such as dunes, salt marshes and mudflats. Where salt marshes and mudflats are unable to retreat inland, they will be 'squeezed' between rising seas and hard defences such as sea walls, and disappear. In the tropics, rising sea levels will threaten coral reefs.

- Shoreline retreats inland.

Human impact

- Increased risks of coastal flooding, especially during periods of spring tide and strong onshore winds. Millions living in poorly defended deltaic areas at sea level in LEDCs (e.g. Bangladesh, Myanmar) are vulnerable.

- Increased rates of erosion both along cliffed coastlines composed of weaker rocks such as clay and gravel, and on lowland coastlines dominated by dunes, salt marshes and mudflats.

- In MEDCs increased investment in hard coastal defences to protect urban areas and key infrastructure such as nuclear power stations and industrial complexes.

- In MEDCs the prohibitive costs of building and maintaining hard coastal defences will result in some sparsely populated coastlines being 'abandoned' to the sea.

> **Typical mistake**
>
> There are two quite separate issues that affect human populations in coastal areas: erosion and flooding. They should not be confused: even though their causes overlap, the human responses are different.

> **Examiner's tip**
>
> It is important to understand the human implications of rising sea level (due to global warming) and to develop a view on the feasibility/ desirability of intervention to limit its impact on human populations.

Case study   Coastal flooding in Eastern England

Causes Low pressure areas or depressions accompanied by gale force winds and high tides occasionally present major flood hazards to the low-lying coastal areas of eastern England. Flooding results from either the breaching of sea defences by elevated sea levels, known as storm surges, or their overtopping by storm waves.

In 1953 a devastating surge was formed by a deep depression that generated hurricane-force winds as it tracked south through the North Sea. As it moved south, the shallow funnel-shape of the southern part of the North Sea amplified its height. The situation was made worse because the storm coincided with an exceptionally high tide. A similar event occurred in November 2007.

Impact Between 31 January and 1 February 1953, eastern England and the southern Netherlands were hit by the greatest North Sea **storm surge** on record. Surge heights reached 3 m at Kings Lynn and 3.36 m in the Netherlands. Flood embankments were breached and sea walls crumbled. In east and southeast England 307 people died, 75,000 ha of farmland were flooded, and 24,000 homes damaged.

In contrast, the 2007 surge was accurately forecast. Flood warnings were issued, the Thames barrier was closed, and people at risk were prepared for evacuation. Fortunately the tidal peak passed without incident, though sea level at Great Yarmouth rose to within 10 cm of the top of the sea walls.

Coastal protection and management

Because of the importance of coasts to human activity, management of the coastal environment to control erosion, flooding, overdevelopment and pollution is essential. There are two approaches to coastal protection and management: hard engineering and soft engineering.

Hard engineering approaches to coastal protection
Revised

Hard engineering has been the standard response to problems of coastal erosion and flooding. It involves the construction of structures such as sea walls, storm surge barriers and groynes (Table 3.4). Increasingly, hard engineering is being questioned because (a) it is economically unsustainable and (b) it has often adverse environmental impact.

Table 3.4 Hard engineering coastal defence structures

Sea walls	Sea walls are expensive to build and maintain. They are only justified where important settlements and/or infrastructure are at risk. Although sea walls stop erosion and prevent flooding they require costly maintenance. By reflecting waves, sea walls generate vertical currents that eventually undermine and topple them. Because sea walls stop erosion they prevent beaches (and mudflats and salt marshes) from migrating inland and accelerate beach erosion. In addition they reduce sediment input to the coastal system by natural erosion which contributes to the narrowing and thinning of beaches.
Revetments	Revetments are wood or rock barriers running parallel to the shoreline. Designed to absorb wave energy they are cheaper than sea walls, but unsightly. They also limit access to beaches for visitors and tourists.
Groynes	Groynes are wood or rock barriers constructed perpendicular to the shoreline. They interrupt the movement of sand and shingle by longshore drift. By keeping beaches intact, they reduce wave erosion. However, they may starve beaches downdrift of sand and shingle and accelerate erosion there.
Rip rap	Rip rap comprises boulders or concrete blocks placed at the foot of cliffs or in the backshore area of a beach. Although unsightly, they are cheap and effective.
Gabions	Gabions are wire cages filled with rocks and shingle. When stacked, they form an effective and cheap defence against coastal erosion.
Barrages	Storm surge barriers such as the Thames and the East Schelde (the Netherlands) barriers protect low-lying estuarine and delta areas from flooding. The capital costs of building (Thames barrier £500 million, East Schelde €1 billion) and operation (East Schelde €17 million a year) are huge. During a period of rising sea level the Thames barrier will be obsolete by the mid-2020s and will need to be replaced.

Examiner's tip

You need to learn the advantages and disadvantages of hard engineering responses to coastal erosion and flooding. The most important issue to address is their economic and environmental sustainability.

Soft engineering approaches to coastal protection
Revised

Soft engineering aims to work *with* natural processes that operate in the coastal system (Table 3.5). As a result it offers a much cheaper alternative to hard engineering which, at the same time, is environmentally sustainable.

Table 3.5 Soft engineering approaches

Beach replenishment	Sand and shingle brought to beaches to replace sediments lost to longshore drift. Beaches are effective absorbers of wave energy, providing the sediment remains *in situ*. Problems may occur if sand for replacement is mined offshore, disrupting the coastal sediment system.
Managed realignment	Existing hard defences may be dismantled or left to fall into disrepair. The shoreline is set back, allowing the sea to flood areas previously protected. Salt marshes, mudflats and beaches develop on the newly flooded areas and provide natural protection against erosion and flooding. This approach is sustainable and has significant environmental benefits (e.g. new inter-tidal habitats for wildlife).
Dune regeneration	Sand fencing and marram planting help to stabilise dunes and reduce wind erosion. Boardwalks laid across the dunes help to discourage trampling by visitors. Brushwood barriers around the high-tide level reduce wave erosion and encourage sand accumulation.
Marsh creation	The creation of salt marshes is a sustainable way of defending lowland coasts from flooding and erosion. Salt marshes raise land levels and dissipate the energy and erosive power of waves. This so-called **managed realignment** of the coast also benefits wildlife, greatly increasing biodiversity.

Exam practice answers and quick quizzes at **www.therevisionbutton.co.uk/myrevisionnotes**

Coastal land use management

In England and Wales, problems of erosion and flooding are the responsibility of local authorities (erosion) and the Environment Agency (flooding). Both problems are coordinated through **shoreline management plans** (SMPs).

Modern coastal management views the coast as an integrated system where, because of the interrelatedness of natural and human systems, change to one part (e.g. stopping erosion) is likely to have adverse knock-on effects elsewhere. As a result, coastal resources and issues such as erosion and flooding are managed together rather than piecemeal.

The basic units of coastal management in England and Wales are the eleven sediment cells (Figure 3.1 on p. 34). SMPs set out a strategy for coastal defence for specified lengths of coast identified within sediment cells known as subcells and management areas.

Two important ideas dominate modern thinking on coastal management:

- human intervention in the natural processes that operate in the coastal zone
  should be minimal
- where intervention is necessary, it should be sustainable

In the past, human intervention in the coastal sediment system has often been disastrous. Meanwhile, the need for sustainable intervention is made more urgent by global warming. Rising sea levels and more frequent storms will place even greater pressure on hard coastal defences in future.

Coastal management in SMPs comprises three strategies:

- *hold the line* — aims to maintain, and in some cases strengthen, existing coastal defences. This policy is justified where the value of properties and infrastructure at risk from erosion and flooding exceeds the cost of defences
- *no active intervention* — covers most of the coastline of England and Wales. Natural processes are allowed to operate without human interference. Sometimes conflicts arise if properties are abandoned to coastal erosion and flooding
- *managed realignment* — setting back the shoreline and allowing the sea to flood areas that were previously protected by embankments and sea walls. Managed realignment has the advantages of (a) reducing the costs of maintaining hard sea defences, (b) allowing salt marshes and mudflats to develop and create natural defences against flooding and erosion, and (c) creating new wildlife habitats such as inter-tidal mudflats and salt marshes.

> **Examiner's tip**
>
> Remember that coastal management policies that may involve the loss of land and property to erosion and flooding are controversial. Case studies, where the pros and cons are clearly set out, need to be learned if you are to address the issues convincingly.

Case study Hard engineering at North Bay, Scarborough

Strengthening hard defences North Bay in Scarborough, surrounded by built-up urban environment, is protected by hard defences. Concrete sea walls extend along the entire length of the Bay and protect the narrow promenade, coastal road and the steep coastal slope. Between 2002 and 2005 the hard sea defences were strengthened in the southern part of the Bay. Thousands of tonnes of rip rap, at a cost of £26 million, were imported by barge and positioned at the foot of the sea wall. The aim was to prevent wave overtopping, damage to infrastructure on the promenade and landslips on the coastal slope.

Issues Hard defences are controversial: apart from their cost, they may have caused significant loss of sediment in the Bay. The advanced line of the defences, and the highly reflective nature of the sea walls may have increased energy levels over the remaining upper beach, resulting in sediment being removed offshore. Without hard defences, North Bay would have a broader upper beach that would provide natural protection for the coast.

Case study   Soft engineering at Freiston Shore, Lincolnshire

Background and issue In 1983, 66 ha of salt marsh at Freiston Shore in Lincolnshire was reclaimed from the sea. The reclaimed land was protected by an earthen flood embankment and converted to arable farming. However, the costs of maintaining the sea defences, together with the relatively low value of the reclaimed land, made managed realignment a more cost-effective, and a more sustainable alternative.

Response and impact A partnership between the Environment Agency, English Nature and the RSPB produced a more sustainable realignment plan which involved the breaching of the flood embankment (2002) allowing the area to return to a mix of salt marsh and saline lagoons. Within 13 months of the breaching the inter-tidal area was colonised by eleven species of salt marsh plants, eight species of fish and numerous waders, geese and ducks. Today, Freiston is an RSPB reserve and attracts nearly 60,000 visitors a year, bringing £150,000 a year to the local economy and creating four full-time jobs.

Now test yourself

11 How does vegetation influence the formation of salt marshes?

12 Name two pioneer species that colonise salt marshes.

13 What is (a) eustatic, (b) isostatic sea level change?

14 How does a marine (a) transgression, (b) regression affect the coastline?

15 What is coastal squeeze?

16 List the three possible strategies in Shoreline Management Plans.

Answers on p. 121

Check your understanding

1 Make a list of the changes to the coastal system induced by sea level rise.

2 Give reasons why some coastlines are dominated by erosional landforms.

3 Explain the role of plants in the formation of dunes and salt marshes.

4 Summarise in a table the main landforms of coastal environments. Classify the landforms according to (a) origin (wave action, wind, tide, weathering, biological) and (b) type (erosional/depositional).

5 Evaluate the hard engineering responses to coastal erosion and coastal flooding.

Answers on p. 121

Exam practice

1 (a) Describe the characteristics of constructive and destructive waves.   [4]

(b) Suggest possible reasons for the difference in gradients between sand and shingle beaches.   [4]

(c) Describe the characteristics of salt marshes and explain their formation.   [7]

(d) With specific reference to case studies of coastal flooding, describe and explain their causes and consequences.   [15]

2 (a) Figure 3.2 shows sediment inputs, stores and transfers in the coastal system. Describe the longshore and offshore/onshore movements of sediment in the coastal system.   [4]

(b) Explain how sediment movements can lead to the formation of coastal dunes.   [4]

(c) Describe and explain the subaerial processes that are likely to be found on cliffed coastlines.   [7]

(d) Explain how sea level change gives rise to the formation of distinctive coastal landforms.   [15]

Answers and quick quiz 3 online

Online

Examiner's summary

✔ The coastal system is driven by the energy of waves, tides and winds. Interaction between energy, geology and sediments occurs through processes of erosion, transport and deposition and gives rise to coastal landforms.

✔ The link between process and form must be clearly established in explanations of coastal erosional and depositional features.

✔ Coastal landforms are dynamic and constantly changing. Some features change within a few hours (e.g. cusps, beach profiles), others change over several decades (e.g. dunes), while cliffs and stacks change on timescales measured in hundreds/thousands of years.

✔ It is inaccurate to relate constructive waves to depositional landforms, and destructive waves to erosional landforms. Constructive waves transfer sediment onshore and build beaches; destructive waves move sediments from beaches offshore and build features such as offshore bars.

✔ Some coastal landforms (e.g. tombolos) are defined by their shape, though they can be formed by different processes (e.g. drift- and swash-aligned features).

✔ It should not be assumed that all cliff coastlines support classic erosional landforms. Boulder clay forms steep cliffs but has insufficient strength and coherence to form caves, arches, stacks etc.

✔ Rather than advancing inland, dunes tend to grow seawards. Older dunes become fixed and immobile as they are colonised by vegetation.

✔ Rising sea level has implications for human activities as well as coastal landforms. It is important to have a clear understanding of the consequences for coastal communities of rising sea level, to appreciate the issues involved and support discussion with specific case studies.

✔ Coastal erosion and flooding may have human consequences that raise issues of management and the extent to which intervention in the natural coastal system is economically and environmentally sustainable.

✔ In England and Wales current coastal management policies favour soft engineering and economically sustainable approaches. When this policy puts people and property at risk it becomes controversial.

✔ Coastal management is about achieving a balance between the costs and benefits of intervention/non-intervention in the coastal system. It is essential to present arguments and evaluate them against criteria such as economic cost, environmental impact and sustainability.

4 Hot deserts and their margins

Location of hot deserts and their margins

Hot deserts and their margins occupy the arid and semi-arid zones in the tropics and subtropics. In the northern hemisphere the arid zone includes the Sahara, Arabian, Gobi and Mojave deserts. In the southern hemisphere it covers most of Australia, and southwest Africa, southern Argentina and northern Chile (Figure 4.1).

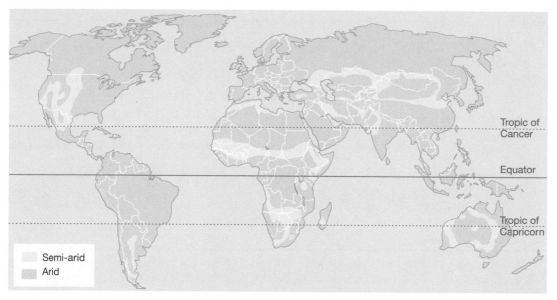

Figure 4.1 World map of aridity

Aridity is defined by the ratio of precipitation (P) to **potential evapotranspiration** (PET). PET is the amount of moisture that, if available, *would be* removed from the land surface by evaporation and transpiration (usually in a year). In the central Sahara, annual precipitation may be less than 3% of PET. In more humid semi-deserts, annual precipitation may reach 50% of PET. Aridity is also influenced by **rainfall effectiveness**, defined as the amount of rain that reaches the root zone in the soil and is available to plants. Apart from rates of evapotranspiration, rainfall effectiveness is related to:

- rainfall **seasonality** — winter rainfall has greater effectiveness than summer rainfall because lower temperatures in winter reduce evapotranspiration losses
- rainfall intensity — rain falling in heavy convectional bursts **runs off** rapidly with little **infiltration** into the soil
- soil type — clay soils have limited capacity to absorb water and therefore create additional runoff. Sandy soils are porous and are highly susceptible to drought

Typical mistake

Aridity is not *just* related to low rainfall. Large parts of eastern England average only 500–600 mm of rainfall per year, but cool conditions mean that the climate is humid.

Examiner's tip

Know that aridity is more than low mean annual rainfall, and that rainfall effectiveness is crucial to understanding plant and crop growth and drought.

Soils

Revised

The soils of hot deserts and their margins are known as **aridisols**. They cover nearly one-third of the Earth's land surface. Several environmental factors limit soil development in arid lands. Most important are slow rates of weathering of parent rocks, and the sparse vegetation cover. Because annual evapotranspiration greatly exceeds annual rainfall, there is little soil **leaching**. This allows mineral ions to accumulate, causing high salinity and alkalinity. Low plant biomass means that the organic content (and therefore nutrient status) of soils is equally low. Aridisols are predominantly mineral soils. They divide into **solonchaks** with a saline **horizon**; and those with a sodium carbonate horizon (**solonetzes**). The resource value of soils for farming in hot deserts and their margins is generally low.

> **Leaching** is the removal of minerals from the soil in solution by rainwater. It results in soil acidity.
>
> Mature soils are differentiated into several layers or **horizons**, defined by their colour, texture, structure and mineral composition.

Vegetation

Revised

Hot deserts and their margins are harsh environments for plants. Plants have to adapt to:

- low and unpredictable rainfall
- low humidity and drying winds
- high summer temperatures
- soils that are deficient in **humus** (dead/decaying organic matter), have low water-holding capacity, lack essential nutrients and have either high salinity or high alkalinity

Desert plants have evolved a number of strategies in order to cope with the problems of low rainfall and drought (Table 4.1). These plants are known as **xerophytes**.

Table 4.1 Adaptations of plants to drought and salinity

Plant type	Adaptation
Succulents	Plants that store water within their tissues (e.g. prickly pear).
Phreatophytes	Plants with long roots to tap water deep below the surface (e.g. tamarisk).
Drought evading	Annual plants that germinate and set seed when it rains. The seeds remain dormant until the next rain (e.g. desert paintbrush).
Dormant	Perennial plants that lie dormant during dry spells and spring to life only when water becomes available.
Halophytes	Plants adapted to survival where salt concentrations are high and toxic to most species (e.g. saltbush). Saltbush stores fresh water in its fleshy leaves.
	Many desert plants survive by reducing water loss by transpiration. Among the water-saving strategies are: shedding leaves, small leaves, leaves whose stomata close during the day, leaves covered in a thick, waxy cuticle, etc.

The causes of aridity

Aridity in the tropics and subtropics is influenced by:

- the **general circulation** of the atmosphere
- topography
- cold ocean currents

General circulation

Revised

Two large convective cells — Hadley cells — control the atmospheric circulation and climate in the tropics. Near the equator intense incoming solar radiation (**insolation**) creates powerful **convection currents**. Warm air rises 10–15 km above the surface and then moves polewards. As it drifts to higher latitudes it cools and, around latitudes 20–30° sinks towards the surface. Warmed by compression this sinking creates cloud-free conditions, and forms a large area of permanent high pressure or **anticyclone** at the surface. This process accounts for the world's largest tropical deserts (e.g. Saharan, Saudi Arabian, Australian).

> **Typical mistake**
>
> Temperature changes are influenced by pressure changes as well as radiation exchanges. Increases in air pressure (as an air parcel descends) result in compression and warming; decreases in pressure (as an air parcel ascends) cause air to expand and cool.

Topography

Revised

Areas to the lee of mountain ranges often lie in a **rain shadow** which can create desert conditions. There are two reasons for this: (1) as **air masses** are forced aloft by mountains, the air cools and expends much of its moisture, (2) air descending on the **leeward slopes** is warmed by compression which lowers its **relative humidity** and reduces the likelihood of rain. Extreme examples of the influence of topography on aridity are: (1) the Kalahari Desert in southern Africa, which lies in the rain shadow of the Drakensberg Mountains in South Africa, and (2) the Mojave Desert in California, isolated from the Pacific Ocean by the Coastal Ranges and Sierra Nevada.

> **Examiner's tip**
>
> To explain the location of deserts fully you need to cite a range of causal factors (i.e. three). Don't forget to give specific examples of deserts in your explanation.

Cold ocean currents

Revised

Cold ocean surface currents flow along the western margins of continents in the tropics and subtropics. They are directly responsible for the formation of coastal deserts in Namibia and northern Chile/southern Peru. In Namibia, the prevailing southeast **trade winds** push surface waters offshore, allowing cold water to upwell from depth. This cold water forms the Benguela current. Meanwhile, air in contact with the ocean surface is chilled and forms a **temperature inversion**. The inversion is spread onshore by local winds, limiting convection and cloud formation. This process, combined with the already dry air caused by (1) the rain shadow effect of the Drakensberg Mountains, and (2) the descent of air to the coast from the African plateau, has created one of the driest environments on the planet — the Namib Desert.

> A **temperature inversion** is an increase in temperature with height, i.e. the reverse of the normal situation in the lower atmosphere.

Now test yourself

1 How is aridity defined?
2 What factors determine rainfall effectiveness?
3 Name three factors that influence the location of hot deserts.
4 Draw an annotated diagram to explain how the circulation of the atmosphere in the tropics and subtropics leads to the formation of hot deserts.
5 Why are cold ocean currents often associated with coastal deserts in the tropics?
6 Explain how mountain ranges create desert and semi-desert conditions.

Answers on p. 122

Weathering

Weathering processes

Revised

Weathering is the *in situ* breakdown of rocks by **mechanical**, chemical and biological processes. The main weathering processes in hot deserts are mechanical, where changes in temperature and moisture cause rocks to break down into smaller particles. Most types of weathering require moisture, and even the driest deserts have occasional rain. In addition moisture is available from **dew** at night. In more humid, semi-arid environments there is usually a wet season which lasts for two or three months.

Rainwater, containing salts in solution, **percolates** into rocks. When the salt crystals precipitate out of solution they exert sufficient pressure to cause rock disintegration. This is **salt weathering**. **Insolation weathering** is the heating of rocks by the Sun. In hot deserts, surface temperatures can range from 80°C in the day to freezing at night. As a result rock minerals expand and contract but at different rates. *Providing* some moisture is present, rocks are weakened and slowly break down.

Freeze–thaw is common in many subtropical desert environments, particularly where altitudes exceed 1,500 m. Clear skies and the relatively thin atmosphere cause significant heat loss at night in winter with temperatures dipping below zero. In these circumstances, water trapped in rock joints and pores freezes, expands as it changes to ice, and causes rock to break down.

> **Typical mistake**
>
> It is wrong to assume that hot deserts have little or no rain. Only in the driest deserts is rainfall exceptionally low as well as erratic and unreliable. Elsewhere, rainfall usually has a seasonal pattern, though drought dominates for most of the year.

The effect of the wind

In desert environments the wind is an active agent of **erosion** and the **transport** and **deposition** of sand, clay and dust. The sparse vegetation cover and dry conditions make wind action more effective than in more humid climates.

> **Typical mistake**
>
> Don't confuse erosion and weathering. Weathering is the *in situ* breakdown of rocks caused by changes of temperature and moisture. Erosion, in contrast, is the wearing away and removal of rocks and rock particles by natural agents such as the wind and running water.

Wind erosion and transport

Revised

The main erosional effect of the wind is the removal of fine particles — a process called **deflation**. Silt and clay-sized particles entrained by the wind can be transported thousands of kilometres. Locally, deflation is responsible for **dust storms** and for surface lowering, which results in shallow depressions and desert surfaces littered with coarse, lag particles. The wind transports sand and silt particles in three ways.

- **Creep** — when sand grains slide and roll across the surface. Creep is caused by drag and by small differences in wind pressure on sand grains that create lift.
- **Saltation** — the downwind skipping motion of sand grains. It occurs only within 1–2 m of the surface. When saltating grains hit a sand surface they have a 'ballistic' effect and set other grains moving in the direction of the wind.
- **Suspension** — small dust particles (less than 2 mm in diameter) can be entrained by the wind and transported in suspension beyond desert areas.

The scouring effect of sand-sized particles saltated by the wind on solid rock is known as **abrasion**. While abrasion can polish rock surfaces, its *overall* impact on desert geomorphology is small. In addition, because sand grains are relatively heavy, the effect of wind abrasion is confined to within just 1–2 m of the surface.

Wind deposition

As winds subside and energy levels fall below the **critical erosion velocity**, the transport of sand, silt and clays ceases and deposition occurs. Sand dunes are the most obvious evidence of sand deposition. Often sand accumulates in areas of reduced wind speed as vast sheets or 'sand seas' known in the Sahara as **ergs**. Once sand is deposited it attracts further deposition because saltating grains are less able to rebound off soft sand compared with hard rocky surfaces.

The effect of water

Sources of rivers

Many desert landforms are the work of streams and rivers. Major perennial rivers, which flow across deserts but derive their waters from more humid regions are known as **exogenous** (e.g. Nile, Colorado). **Endoreic** rivers have catchments wholly within deserts and their margins (e.g. Okovango). They are often seasonal and flow to inland lakes and basins. Short-lived, **ephemeral streams** and rivers only flow after heavy rain. Ephemeral streams form dry river channels called **wadis** or arroyos.

Role of flooding

Although draining relatively small catchments, ephemeral streams and rivers often have high **peak flows** and, for a short time, extreme power. High peak flows are due to: sparse vegetation cover and therefore little interception of rainfall; impermeable ground surfaces, baked hard by the Sun; and shallow soils. Intense rainfall events such as thunderstorms also give rise to rapid runoff, high peak flows and flooding. During these events, ephemeral streams and rivers are powerful agents of erosion and transport.

> **Examiner's tip**
>
> Appreciate that water, although absent from deserts for most of the time, is nonetheless a highly effective agent of landscape change in desert environments.

Desert landforms

Desert landforms are due to the action of wind, water and weathering.

The effect of wind

Yardangs and zeugens

Yardangs are streamlined ridges of solid rock, aligned in the direction of the prevailing wind. They can reach 100 m in height. They are often undercut at the base — evidence that abrasion by saltating sand grains is involved in their formation. **Zeugens** develop where harder horizontally bedded rocks rest on weaker strata. The weaker rock is undercut by wind abrasion, causing the more resistant strata to survive as tabular ridges, up to 30 m high. The term zeugen is also used to describe a range of curiously shaped rocks (e.g. pedestal or mushroom rocks) attributed to wind erosion.

Dunes

Dunes are mounds and ridges of blown sand. Two conditions are needed for dune formation: (1) an adequate supply of sand and (2) winds strong enough and persistent enough to transport the sand.

A typical dune has a windward slope of 10–15°, a sharp crest and a much steeper leeward or slip face of 30–35° (Figure 4.2). The slip face stands at the angle of repose, i.e. the maximum angle at which loose sand is stable. Creep and saltation transport sand up the windward slope. As sand accumulates on the crest it eventually exceeds the angle of repose, causing small avalanches down the slip face which restores equilibrium. In this way dunes advance in the direction of the prevailing wind.

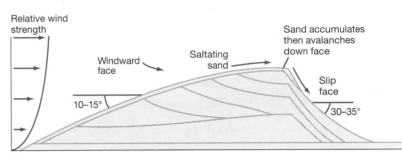

Figure 4.2 Formation of desert dunes

Types of dune

There are four main types of dune, classified according to their shape in planform (Figure 4.3). Several factors influence dune types, including sand supply, wind direction and vegetation cover.

Crescentic dunes are wider than they are long, with slip faces on their concave side. The two main types of crescentic dune are **barchans** and **transverse dunes**. Barchans are easily recognised by horns that face downwind. They form where winds blow predominantly from one direction. Like barchans, transverse dunes develop at right angles to the prevailing wind but are a feature of large erg environments and can be several hundred metres high. All crescentic dunes are highly mobile, moving up to 100 m in a year.

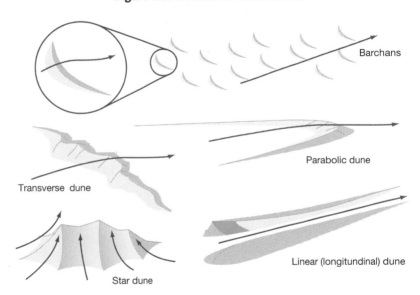

Figure 4.3 Dune types

Linear dunes are straight or slightly curved in planform. They are often more than 100 km long with slip faces on alternate sides. They occur either as isolated or parallel ridges and cover a larger area of desert than any other dune type. **Star dunes** are pyramidal in profile with slip faces on three or more arms that radiate from a dome-line summit. They form in areas where the wind is multidirectional.

Parabolic dunes have U-shaped planforms with convex noses trailed by elongated arms. Unlike crescentic dunes, these arms extend upwind. The arms are fixed by vegetation while the main mass of the dune moves forward.

> **Typical mistake**
>
> It is a mistake to think that most hot deserts comprise sand seas and dunes. Only about one-fifth of the Earth's hot deserts are covered with sand. Rocky, stony surfaces are more common.

The effect of water

Pediments, mesas and buttes

Pediments are gently sloping rock platforms found at the base of mountain fronts in hot deserts and their margins. Widespread in arid lands, they are often covered with a veneer of alluvium and coarse sediment. Isolated rocky hills and mountains, known as **inselbergs**, often rise abruptly from pediment surfaces.

Both pediments and inselbergs develop from the **parallel retreat** of the steep slopes of plateaux or mountain fronts. As the slopes retreat (mainly due to weathering and rockfall) they leave behind a gently angled rock platform or pediment. Parallel retreat, over millions of years, gives more or less constant slope profiles to mountain fronts in arid lands. On the Colorado Plateau at Monument Valley in Arizona and Utah, parallel retreat has reduced the ancient sandstone plateau to remnant tablelands known as **mesas** and **buttes** (Figure 4.4).

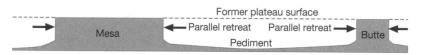

Figure 4.4 Mesas and buttes

Alluvial fans

Alluvial fans are cones of debris that accumulate along mountain fronts. They form when a river leaves a steep-walled valley (canyon) in the mountains and enters an adjacent basin or lowland. On entering the basin the reduction in gradient causes a sudden loss of energy and the deposition of alluvium. The main channel splits into hundreds of smaller channels, creating a delta-shaped mound of debris with a shallow gradient and concave profile in section. Where multiple alluvial fans develop they often merge to form a continuous apron of debris known as a **bajada**.

Salt lakes

Most streams and rivers in hot deserts and their margins drain to shallow inland basins where they form temporary lakes or **playas**. The lakes soon evaporate, leaving behind salts such as sodium chloride, sodium sulphate and gypsum. In more humid environments these salts would normally be transported to the sea. In deserts they accumulate to form extensive salt flats such as those at Badwater in Death Valley (California).

Badlands

In hot deserts and their margins, large areas of softer rocks such as shale and siltstone are often carved into dense networks of parallel V-shaped rills and gulleys. These channels are usually separated by narrow knife-edged ridges. This is badland topography. A major cause of **badlands** is the absence of vegetation and soil, with resulting large-scale runoff and fluvial erosion.

Now test yourself

7 What are the main weathering processes in hot deserts and their margins?

8 Outline what is meant by wind erosion and wind transport.

9 How do sand creep, saltation and suspension contribute to wind transport?

10 Explain the formation of (a) one erosional landform, (b) one depositional landform found in hot deserts and their margins.

Answers on p. 122

Desertification

What is desertification?

Desertification is the degradation of formerly productive land to the point where desert-like conditions prevail. There is a gradual loss of biological and economic activity as water, soil and vegetation resources are exhausted. One-third of the Earth's land surface is threatened by desertification, directly affecting 250 million people. Annually an estimated 1.5–2.5 million ha of irrigated land and 3.5–4.0 million ha of rain-fed agricultural land lose all or part of their productivity through desertification.

Fragile desert environments
Revised

Hot deserts and their margins are fragile environments, easily degraded by human activity. Their fragility is due to:

- low rates of primary production and plant growth caused by sparse rainfall and high temperatures
- low biodiversity — with few species adapted to the harsh desert environments, the loss of a single species can destabilise and degrade entire ecosystems

> **Typical mistake**
>
> Do not assume that desertification always results in desert-like conditions. Desertification usually means something far less dramatic, such as reductions in plant/crop/livestock production, deforestation, accelerated soil erosion, etc.

Causes of desertification
Revised

Desertification is due to a combination of physical and human factors. Drought certainly plays a part. Low and variable rainfall is a diagnostic feature of hot desert and semi-desert climates. While ecosystems and indigenous human groups are adapted to seasonal and erratic rainfall, prolonged droughts can cause devastation. Vital natural resources such as water, soil and woodland gradually degrade, sometimes to the point where ecosystems collapse and recovery is impossible.

Human populations and human activities also play a critical role in desertification. In the Sahel, rapid population growth among cultivators and pastoralists has put enormous strain on the physical environment. Niger's population for example, doubled between 1990 and 2010 to over 16 million. As the demand for food and water surged, desperate farmers resorted to getting more out of the land, resulting in **overcultivation**, overirrigation and overgrazing. At the same time woodlands were cleared to provide fuelwood for cooking and heating and to extend the frontier of cultivation.

> **Examiner's tip**
>
> Examiners look for (a) a balanced understanding of the causes of desertification, and (b) an appreciation that desertification often results from the interaction between human factors (e.g. population growth), drought and climate change.

The impact of desertification
Revised

Desertification has a degrading impact on the land, ecosystems and people.

Land

The most visible impact of land degradation is the dramatic loss of topsoil to wind and surface runoff. The main triggers of **soil erosion** are deforestation, caused by overgrazing or deliberate clearance for fuelwood and timber; and overcultivation, which depletes the soil's organic matter and destroys its **structure**. Soil erosion also results in secondary problems, which include: damage to crops by blown soil, slopes carved by deep gullies, and the siltation of irrigation canals and reservoirs.

> **Soil erosion** is the accelerated loss of topsoil due to human mismanagement.

Salinisation occurs when salts accumulate in the soil at levels that are toxic to crops. Most salinisation is due to overirrigation and poor drainage. The outcome is a rise in the water table until salty water reaches the root zone of crops. In extreme cases water is drawn to the surface by capillary action where it evaporates and leaves behind a saline crust.

Ecosystems

Drought and population growth place acute pressure on ecosystems in hot deserts and their margins. The destruction of woodlands (**deforestation**) for firewood for cooking and lighting has hastened desertification in west African countries such as Burkina Faso, Mali and Niger. In some places, virtually all trees have been removed for several kilometres around settlements. Meanwhile, overgrazing by livestock prevents regeneration. **Deforestation** exposes fragile soils to erosion by wind and water. Competition for grazing and browsing by domestic livestock also impacts adversely on wild animal populations, especially larger herbivores such as antelope. As a result, food webs collapse, ecosystems degrade and plant productivity and biodiversity decline.

People

Land degradation reduces the productive potential of farmland and therefore impoverishes the lives of millions of people. In extreme cases it leads to food shortages and to permanent damage to soil, water and vegetation resources. Societies that for centuries have maintained a delicate balance between the use and regeneration of local resources, become **unsustainable**. With the land producing less, and with more mouths to feed, a vicious cycle of decline is set in motion. The ultimate outcomes are reduced **food security** and an increase in food shortages and **famines**. Eventually people may be forced to abandon degraded areas and seek refuge in towns and cities.

> **Typical mistake**
>
> Often there is a failure to appreciate that indigenous groups have developed systems to cope with drought. Crises develop when the problem of rapid population growth is superimposed on prolonged drought lasting years or even decades.

> **Examiner's tip**
>
> Examiners will credit an understanding that famine rarely means an absolute food shortage in a society. Famine often hits one sector of society — usually the poorest — who have the fewest entitlements (e.g. land, savings) and the lowest level of food security.

Case study Desertification in Nara, the Sahel

Background Nara in Mali occupies the Sahel, a vast semi-arid region on the southern fringes of the Sahara Desert in Africa that stretches from Senegal to Eritrea. Mean annual rainfall in the Sahel is around 375 mm but PET is four to five times greater. Rainfall is also highly seasonal with a short wet season between June and October. The rest of the year is dry. Ecosystems and indigenous societies are adapted to periodic droughts. Indigenous societies fall into two groups: (1) agro-pastoralists (e.g. Sarakolé), who are sedentary, and (2) nomadic pastoralists (e.g. Fulani).

Desertification — causes and effects Desertification began when severe drought hit the Sahel between 1969 and 1974. Since then, average rainfall has fallen by 30%. At the same time, the human population has grown rapidly, causing demand for food, fodder for livestock and firewood have risen steeply. Drought and population growth have placed a huge strain on environmental resources, leading to deforestation,

overgrazing and overcultivation. As a result crop yields have declined, food shortages have become more common and poverty has increased. Many local people can no longer survive on the land and have migrated to the capital, Bamako.

There is no tradition of managing pastureland in Nara. Consequently grazing has been uncontrolled and pasture quality has declined. In response to population pressure, agro-pastoralists have extended cultivation into marginal areas at the expense of woodland. Shortages of pasture have caused conflict between nomadic groups and agro-pastoralists. Meanwhile drought has increased the salt content of groundwater and overgrazing has threatened biodiversity. Wildlife such as rabbits and antelope, once an important food source, have largely disappeared, while years of plentiful rain (2003, 2004) have brought further misery, triggering plagues of locusts that devastated crops.

Managing hot deserts and their margins

Physical limits to plant growth set by low rainfall mean that farmland and ecosystems recover only slowly from the effects of desertification in hot deserts and their margins. Management responses vary depending on levels of economic development. They include: reafforestation programmes, land drainage, destocking to reduce the grazing pressure, irrigation, and education of farmers in techniques of sustainable land management.

Responses in LEDCs   Revised ☐

Case study Reafforestation in northern China

Desertification and environmental degradation
One-third of China's total land area suffers desertification and environmental degradation. The arid and semi-arid regions of northern China such as the Korqin Sandy Lands are most badly affected. Strong winds are the main agents of desertification and produce violent dust storms. Desertification is also due to overgrazing and deforestation, both driven by human population growth.

Rehabilitation scheme In 1978 China embarked on an ambitious programme to combat desertification in its northern provinces. The scheme, popularly known as the 'great green wall' is a massive reafforestation programme. It aims to create 350,000 km^2 of new forests and shelterbelts by 2050. In Korqin, the programme will protect farmland against erosion, restore soil fertility and improve the incomes of local

inhabitants. It will also provide a sustainable source of timber.

The scheme is not just about reafforestation. It also includes: conservation, with the introduction of sustainable cultivation involving the recycling of organic material to the soil; the integration of tree crops with pasture and cash crops (agro-forestry); planting tree species (e.g. native poplars) that provide fodder as well as timber and improve soil fertility; controlled management of grazing lands in balance with the **carrying capacity**.

> **Carrying capacity** is the number of stock per unit area that grazing land can support sustainably.

Case study The reclamation of salinised land in northern Pakistan

Salinisation By the late 1980s, overirrigation had caused severe problems of waterlogging and salinisation of farmland in the semi-arid district of Khushab in northern Pakistan. As crop yields fell and farmland was abandoned, unemployment soared.

Response The problems were addressed by a project funded by the World Bank to reclaim 360 km^2 of degraded farmland. It also aimed to increase agricultural production, create more jobs and raise farmers' incomes. Rehabilitating the land involved underdrainage using PVC pipes, the construction of new surface water drains and lining irrigation canals.

In addition, farmers were educated in practices of sustainable water management.

Outcome The project, completed in 1994, proved highly successful. Groundwater levels were lowered and waterlogging and soil salinity reduced. Improvements in land quality increased the production of crops such as rice, wheat and sugar cane. Per capita incomes of farming families also increased from US$46 in 1989 to US$195 in 2005. Without the project the World Bank estimated that average incomes would have continued to decline to around US$30.

Farming and livestock integration In the western Sahel — in Niger, Mali and Burkina Faso — development agencies from North America and Europe have successfully tackled problems of desertification by integrating farming and livestock herding. Key to success was:

- the introduction of planned systems of rotation
- the use of crop residues for livestock forage
- the recycling of nutrients by livestock grazed for part of the year on croplands

Outcome These methods raised outputs of food and fodder crops and reduced the need to extend cultivation onto open pastureland. In the past, this practice not only placed remaining pastures under even greater pressure and but also led to conflict between farming and pastoral groups. Rotation has now been extended to wild pastures: instead of continuous grazing, the open pastures have been divided into subzones, each grazed for two weeks at a time. The results have been positive: the productivity and health of livestock have improved, conflicts between farmers and herders have been resolved, and a sustainable system of farming has been established.

Examiner's tip

Examiners want to see students (a) use case studies detailing the human responses to desertification, and (b) evaluate the effectiveness of these responses. The latter can be measured against various criteria: economic — impact on incomes and living standards; ecological — impact on water, soils, vegetation etc.; sustainability — the ability of local people to operate the scheme in the long term.

Responses in MEDCs

Revised

Water supply from the Colorado Basin

Much of the US southwest, covering large parts of southern California, Nevada and Arizona, is desert and semi-desert. In a largely waterless region, economic development has relied heavily on water extracted from the exogenous Colorado River. Water stored in a series of massive dams (Figure 4.5) is shared between states in the Colorado Basin through the Colorado River Compact (1922), and delivered through a network of aqueducts to areas of consumption. Colorado water supplies a number of major cities in the southwest, including Las Vegas, Phoenix, Scottsdale and Tuscon. These massive water transfer schemes involve huge capital expenditure and are only feasible in rich countries. Despite rapid urban growth, agriculture is by far the biggest water consumer. Water from the Colorado irrigates 200,000 ha in California's Imperial Valley and 500,000 ha in southern Arizona, transforming the desert into vast green oases. Although Colorado water is supplemented by local groundwater, the growth of desert cities such as Las Vegas and Phoenix and their booming economies would be impossible without water from the Colorado River.

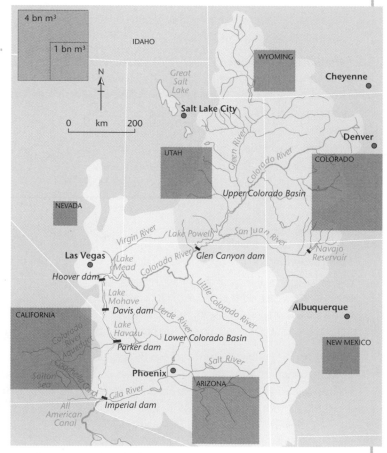

Figure 4.5 Colorado drainage basin and water allotments by state

Future water demand and sustainability The pace of economic growth in the US southwest in the past 40 years has been unprecedented. However, the region is beginning to run out of water. For some years Las Vegas, whose population more than doubled between 1990 and 2009, has been desperately searching for new sources of groundwater in the desert to the north of the city. Similar problems affect Phoenix, which experienced a two-thirds population increase between 1990 and 2009. Without new sources of water, current rates of economic and population growth will not be sustainable in the arid US southwest in future.

Now test yourself

11 Why are desert environments described as 'fragile'?

12 What is desertification?

13 Name and explain one physical and one human factor which cause desertification.

14 State three adverse effects of desertification on resources for farming in hot deserts and their margins.

15 Describe two methods that can be used to reverse the effects of desertification.

16 Describe a sustainable system of farming in hot deserts and their margins.

Answers on p. 122

Check your understanding

1 Describe and explain how plants in hot desert environments have adapted to drought.

2 Describe the action of running water in hot deserts and their margins and explain its effectiveness as a geomorphological agent.

3 Summarise in a table the main landforms found in desert areas. Classify the landforms according to (a) origin (wind action or water action), (b) type (erosional/depositional).

4 Construct a flow diagram to explain the causes and consequences of desertification.

Answers on p. 122

Exam practice

1 (a) Amplify the view that aridity is more than low mean annual rainfall. [4]

(b) Study Figure 4.1 which shows the global distribution of arid climates. Describe the distribution of arid climates in the tropics and subtropics. [4]

(c) Explain how the atmospheric circulation and ocean currents influence aridity in the tropics and subtropics. [7]

(d) With reference to contrasting case studies, evaluate the success of management strategies aimed at achieving sustainable agriculture and land use in arid environments. [15]

2 (a) Describe the main types of mechanical weathering found in hot deserts and their margins. [4]

(b) Suggest reasons why wind erosion and transport are important landforming processes in hot deserts and their margins. [4]

(c) Study Figure 4.4 which shows mesas, buttes and pediments in an arid environment. Describe and explain the formation of the landforms in Figure 4.4.

(d) 'Hot desert environments are fragile and easily degraded by human activity.' Discuss the validity of this statement.

Answers and quick quiz 4 online

Online

Examiner's summary

✔ Annotated diagrams and sketch maps are often more appropriate than text per se to explain landforms and the causes of deserts.

✔ Successful explanations of desert landforms require you to make a specific connection between processes and form.

✔ It is the interaction of rainfall and evapotranspiration that explains the formation of most deserts, not low rainfall alone.

✔ Desertification affects both rich and poor countries. Case studies of desertification should reflect this.

✔ Examiners will credit candidates who understand that famine is not just an absolute food shortage, and that

famine often hits the poorest members of society hardest, i.e. those with fewest entitlements (e.g. land, savings) and the lowest level of food security.

✔ Desertification is a complex process that involves several variables. Answers in the examination should convey this complexity.

✔ Examiners welcome student answers that (a) use case studies detailing the human responses to problems such as desertification, and (b) evaluate the effectiveness of these responses to desertification against economic, environmental and sustainability criteria.

5 Population change

Population indicators

At the global scale, the number of births and deaths influence population change. If births outnumber deaths, the global population expands. This is **natural increase**. When deaths exceed births, the population declines and there is **natural decrease**. At continental, national, regional and local scales a third factor, **migration**, affects population change.

Measuring fertility
Revised

Fertility is the occurrence of live births. Many factors influence fertility including economic status, religion, government policies, female literacy, the economic value of children and the availability of contraceptive devices. In most societies fertility falls when economic development increases.

Crude birth rate

The **crude birth rate** (CBR) is widely used as a measure of fertility. The CBR is the ratio of the number of live births to the total population and is usually expressed per 1,000 of the population per year. As a measure of fertility, the CBR has drawbacks because it is strongly influenced by the age–sex structure. Regardless of how many children each woman produces, aged populations and populations with relatively few women will have low CBRs.

General fertility rate

The **general fertility rate** is the number of live births in a year as a ratio of the number of women aged 15–44, expressed per 1,000 women. In 2009 the general fertility rate in England and Wales was 63.7 per 1,000.

Total fertility rate

The total fertility rate (TFR) is the average number of live births to women who have completed their families. The reproductive TFR (i.e. the rate needed just to replace the population) is 2.1.

> **Typical mistake**
>
> It is often assumed that the CBR is an accurate indicator of fertility. This is not so. For instance, CBRs are high where a large proportion of women are in the reproductive age groups (15–45), even though each woman on average may have just two or three children.

Measuring mortality
Revised

Mortality is the occurrence of death. Rates of mortality depend on many factors such as age, diet, healthcare, economic status and disease. In general, mortality declines over time as living standards rise. There are several measures of mortality.

Crude death rate

The **crude death rate** (CDR) is the number of deaths per 1,000 of the population per year and has similar disadvantages to the CBR.

Age-specific mortality

Age-specific mortality is the number of deaths per 1,000 in specific age groups per year. In developed countries it generally peaks in infancy and then declines until the mid-teens. Thereafter, there is a slow increase until extreme old age, when the rate rises steeply.

Infant mortality rate

The **infant mortality rate** (IMR) is the number of deaths of children under 1 year old per 1,000 live births. The IMR is a particularly sensitive indicator of the standard of living in a society.

Life expectancy

Life expectancy is the average life span of an individual at birth. It is influenced by a range of factors, including healthcare, diet, lifestyle, economic status, gender and so on. Life expectancy increases with economic development and wealth. In 2009 in the UK life expectancy was 82 years for women and 78 years for men. In comparison, life expectancy in the UK in 1900 was 51 years for women and 48 years for men.

Vital rates and population change
Revised

The CBR and CDR — also known as **vital rates** — are used to calculate natural population change. In the absence of any migration, the percentage natural population change per year is equal to:

> % natural change = (CBR per 1,000 − CDR per 1,000)/10

Using this formula, in 2010 India, with vital rates of 21 (CBR) and 8 (CDR), has a natural increase rate of 13 per 1,000 or 1.3% per year.

Typical mistake

Migration is a population movement that implies a degree of permanence. As a result, temporary movements such as commuting and tourist trips are not classed as migrations.

Measuring migration
Revised

Migration is the permanent or semi-permanent movement of people from one place to another. **Net migration** is the difference in numbers of in-migrants and out-migrants over a given period, e.g. 1 year. When in-migrants exceed out-migrants, there is a **net migrational gain**. A **net migrational loss** occurs when there is an excess of out-migrants over in-migrants. Migration, together with fertility and mortality, determines population change (and population structure) at continental, national, regional and local scales.

Examiner's tip

Any analysis of the impact of migration on a society should include net migration. Net migration is a major determinant of population change at regional and local scales.

The demographic transition

The demographic transition model
Revised

The **demographic transition model** (DTM) originally described the shift from high fertility and mortality to low fertility and mortality that occurred in Europe's population between 1750 and 1950. As Figure 5.1 shows, the transition comprised five stages and was accompanied by economic growth and rising living standards.

- Stage 1 — Pre-industrial. Fertility and mortality (and vital rates) are high. There is little population growth. High fertility is needed to ensure the survival of the population. Children also provide a source of labour and security for parents in old age. Artificial contraception is unavailable. High mortality is due to poor nutrition, poor hygiene and lack of medical knowledge to combat disease.

- Stages 2 and 3 — Industrial. Improvements in medicine and in economic, social and environmental conditions cause mortality rates (and death rates) to fall. In stage 2, fertility remains high and results in rapid population growth. The fertility decline evident in stage 3 lags behind mortality decline. Even so, the rate of population increase begins to slow. Fertility decline occurs because: children become expensive (long education period), the state provides for security in old age, artificial contraception is available, and infant mortality is low so that few children die in infancy.

- Stage 4 — Post-industrial. Both fertility and mortality (and vital rates) are low. Population growth is either very slow or has ceased altogether. Further causes of low fertility include: women postponing marriage until their mid- to late-twenties, more educated women with high-status jobs, more unmarried couples living together who are less likely to have children than married couples, and more effective methods of birth control.

- Stage 5 — Declining. The trend of declining fertility and birth rates continues. As the population ages the CBR falls below the CDR resulting, for the first time, in natural population decrease.

> **Examiner's tip**
>
> It is important to recognise that the DTM is based on population changes that occurred in western Europe between 1800 and 1950. Its application to other parts of the world with very different cultural and economic contexts is contentious.

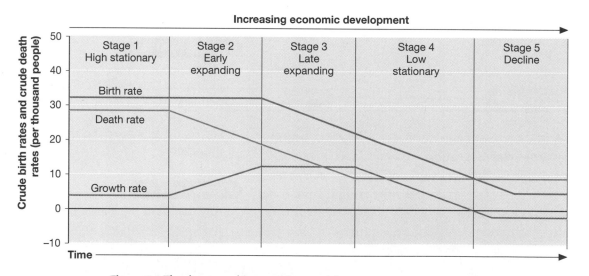

Figure 5.1 The demographic transition model

Evaluating the demographic transition model
Revised

The DTM does not appear to describe accurately the experiences of most developing countries in the past 50 or 60 years. There are several possible reasons for this.

- Absolute numbers of population increase and growth rates have been much higher in developing countries than in nineteenth-century Europe. No countries in Europe ever had annual population growth rates of more than 1%.

- Mortality decline was a gradual process in nineteenth-century Europe. It followed improvements in living conditions brought about by economic growth and advances in tackling diseases such as smallpox. In developing countries, mortality decline has been more rapid. This decline is due largely to the application of modern medical techniques rather than to progress in living standards. In some countries, such as China and Bangladesh, government policies have increased the rate of population change. In southern Africa, the HIV/AIDS epidemic has caused an exceptional increase in mortality.

- Most developing countries are less urbanised than nineteenth-century Europe. The economic advantages of large families in rural societies, low levels of literacy (particularly among women) and the strength of traditional values and cultures, have all proved obstacles to lowering fertility levels in developing countries.

Now test yourself

1 What are vital rates?
2 Name three demographic factors that determine population change in a city or region.
3 Why is the crude birth rate not an accurate indicator of fertility?
4 Define the terms: life expectancy, migration, net migrational change.
5 Make a sketch of the DTM. Insert labels and annotations on your sketch to describe the five stages of the demographic transition.

Answers on p. 123

Population structure

Population structure describes the composition of a population according to age and gender.

Population pyramids

Revised

Population structure is represented by a special kind of bar chart known as a **population pyramid**. Some examples are shown in Figure 5.2. Several factors influence the shape of population pyramids. Some are short term, such as wars, epidemics and famines; others, such as fertility and mortality control, have a long-term effect. These long-term influences give rise to distinctive pyramid shapes.

- Broad-based pyramids, such as those for Pakistan and Indonesia in Figure 5.2, show youthful populations with large proportions of children and high levels of fertility. These pyramids are typical of less economically developed countries (**LEDCs**) in stage 2 of the demographic transition. If fertility increases over time, the pyramid is **progressive**. Some pyramids show the effects of high fertility in the past. An unusually large birth cohort may follow a 'baby boom', such as occurred in western Europe at the end of the Second World War (e.g. Germany, Figure 5.2). Today, these countries have large proportions of older adults aged between 55 and 65 years.

- Rapidly tapering pyramids, such as those for Pakistan and Indonesia in Figure 5.2, suggest high levels of mortality, with significant reductions in numbers at each 5-year age group. These populations usually have only small proportions of old people — hence their narrow apex. Again, these pyramids are typical of LEDCs in stage 2 of the demographic transition.

- Straight-sided pyramids, with little reduction in the size of age groups between 0 and 60 years, suggest both low fertility and low mortality. More economically developed countries (**MEDCs**) have this type of pyramid, which is therefore typical of stages 4 and 5 of the demographic transition.

- Pyramids with a narrow base that broadens with age, such as that for Germany in Figure 5.2, indicate recent reductions in fertility. These pyramids are known as **regressive**. Many LEDCs in stage 3 of the demographic transition which have experienced sharp reductions in fertility in recent years (e.g. China, Malaysia) have regressive pyramids.

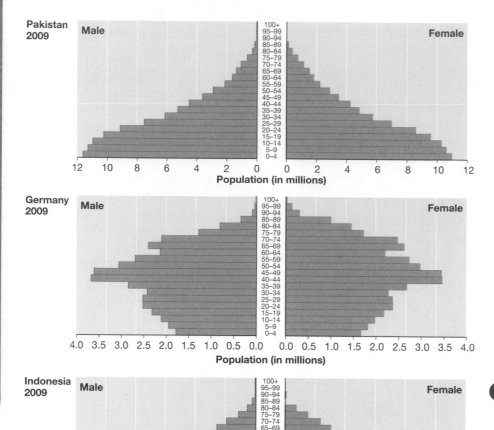

Figure 5.2 Population pyramids: (a) Pakistan, (b) Germany and (c) Indonesia, 2009

Population structure and migration

Revised

Migration has most effect on population structure at a local and regional scale. This is because migration is both age and sex **selective**. In most societies, the majority of migrants are young adults. Therefore, places of recent net migrational gain often have more young adults than average, while those suffering a net migrational loss have fewer. The migrational effects of gender are more variable. In southern Africa, males migrate more often than females, giving unbalanced sex ratios both in receiving (usually urban) and sending (usually rural) areas. In South America, the situation is reversed, with females more likely to migrate than males.

Population change: economic, social and political implications

Revised

The age–sex structure of a population has important implications for the balance between people and resources at local, regional and national scales.

● Most LEDCs have youthful populations with between 30% and 45% aged 15 and younger. With so many children entering young adulthood, even with declining fertility, rapid population growth is inevitable in future. This means greater demands on resources such as food, energy, education and healthcare.

● At a regional scale, migrational change often unbalances age–sex structures.

In rural areas most out-migrants are young adults. The result is fewer babies and a general **ageing** of the rural population. This has implications for the viability of essential services such as schools and public transport. Destinations that attract young adult migrants (i.e. cities) experience the opposite effects: net in-migration inflates the reproductive age groups and increases rates of population growth and demands for housing, services and other resources.

- Ageing also occurs in communities in MEDCs that attract retirees. In the UK, the south coast is a popular retirement area, leading to ageing populations in towns such as Eastbourne and Christchurch. This process affects demand for local services such as schools (decline) and healthcare (increase).

- Ageing at the national scale reduces the relative size of the workforce and increases the proportion of old people. The result is greater economic **dependency** of the older (non-working) population on the **economically active.** Problems of 'greying' populations and increasing dependency are widespread in MEDCs.

- In MEDCs the economically active population comprises adults between the ages of 18 and 65 years. Already, low fertility in these countries in the past 50 or 60 years has resulted in sluggish population growth at best (Japan's population actually declined between 2005 and 2010). This trend raises concerns about labour shortages and declining tax revenues (Figure 5.3). It also has implications for the economy and for the provision of healthcare services and state pensions for retired people. Solving this problem has become a political as well as an economic issue.

- In LEDCs high fertility has led to ever-increasing numbers of children and soaring demand for healthcare and educational services. Once again the result is imbalance in the population structure and increased dependency.

Examiner's tip

For every society there will be a theoretical optimal population size and structure. Definitions of 'optimal population' might include: the population size/ structure that maximises resources per person, or is economically and/or environmentally sustainable in the long term etc.

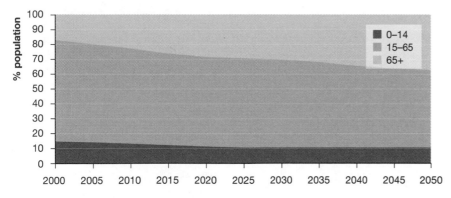

Figure 5.3 Japan's ageing population, 2000–2050

Managing population change Revised

Many governments seek to manage population change. Population policies in LEDCs most often focus on the problem of rapid population growth. Policies that aim to reduce growth by lowering fertility are known as **anti-natalist**. A few countries (e.g. Malaysia) have **pro-natalist** policies designed to encourage fertility and increase population growth. Governments can also influence population change either by encouraging or limiting international in-migration. Such policies are most often adopted by MEDCs.

Case study **China's population policy**

Background China's anti-natalist population policy was a response to perceived overpopulation in the 1970s. Between 1950 and 1980 China's population increased from 560 to 985 million. Such growth threatened shortages of food, fresh water, fossil fuels and other natural resources. As a communist country, China gives priority to state interests over the rights and freedom of individuals. Therefore, the government was able to impose an authoritarian policy that would be impossible in democratic societies.

The policy China introduced its one-child policy in 1979. Women who opted to have more than one child incurred economic penalties. The legal age for marriage was increased to 22 years for men and 20 years for women. The policy was applied with greater flexibility in rural than in urban areas. Even in urban areas there has recently been some policy relaxation. For example, if a couple were themselves both only children, they could try for a second child 4 years after the birth of their first child.

Impact The policy had most success in towns and cities, where it was easier to enforce and where small families were more acceptable. In rural areas the policy met more resistance: it was difficult both to enforce and to explain to poorly educated farmers.

The overall impact of the policy has been dramatic. Whereas the country's population increased by 73% between 1950 and 1979, growth fell to 37% between 1979 and 2008. Today, one-third of all Chinese families are single-child families. It is claimed that the policy has been responsible for 400 million fewer births.

However, the policy has greatly altered China's age structure and will create economic and social problems in future.

- The proportion of young people has fallen steeply, threatening labour shortages in cities.
- Thanks to improvements in healthcare and living standards, the proportion of old people has risen, increasing levels of dependency. Although only 9% of China's population was aged 60 years and over in the early 1990s, by 2030 the proportion will reach 25%. With little state provision for pensions the burden of looking after old people will fall on today's single child.
- The preference for male children has led to female infanticide and selective abortions of girls. The resulting gender imbalance will eventually mean a shortage of marriageable women, threatening the tradition of universal marriage.

Case study **Immigration to the UK: 2004–2007**

Recent immigration trends There was an annual net migration gain in the UK for most of the period 1990–2007. Before 2004, most immigration originated from Africa, the Middle East and south Asia. Since the enlargement of the EU in 2004, the majority of immigrants have come from EU countries in eastern Europe. Between 2004 and 2006, 181,000 immigrants entered the UK from eastern Europe. In 2007 the overall net migration gain was

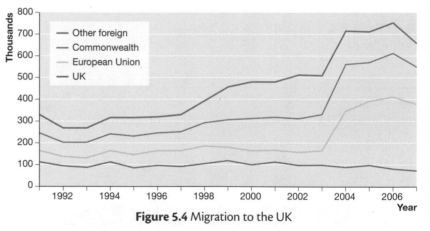

Figure 5.4 Migration to the UK

237,000. Immigration reached record levels between 2000 and 2010 and is currently the main driver of population growth (Figure 5.4).

Causes Immigration has been driven by a combination of economic push and pull factors. In 2007, GNI per capita in the UK was US$40,660, compared with US$9,850 in Poland; unemployment in Poland in March 2007 was twice as high as in the UK; and the minimum wage in the UK was more than five times greater. Citizens of other EU countries have a legal right to live and work in the UK.

Successive UK governments have encouraged immigration because most in-migrants are young adults and are economically active. They help to counter problems of an ageing population and rising dependency. Immigrants provided a source of skilled and relatively cheap labour which the British economy needed in the economic boom years of 2004–2007.

Impact A report by the Select Committee for Economic Affairs in 2008 suggested that the overall benefits of immigration to the UK economy had been exaggerated and that the economic benefits depend on the skills of the immigrants. Large numbers of young immigrants with families, for example, can put a strain on housing and public services such as schools and healthcare. There are also environmental concerns over rising population pressure, with ever-increasing demands for housing and the loss of countryside to urban development.

6 Sketch the main characteristics of progressive and regressive population pyramids.

7 In what ways is migration a selective process?

8 What is meant by an ageing population and what are its economic implications for a population or country?

9 Why does migration often contribute to an increase in dependency in (a) rural, (b) urban communities?

10 What are the differences between pro-natalist and anti-natalist population policies?

Answers on p. 123

The impact of population change in urban and rural areas

Causes of urban and rural population change

Revised

Population change in urban and rural areas is due to a combination of natural change and migration. In the developing world, **urbanisation** is occurring rapidly. Natural increase accounts for around 60% of annual urban population growth in LEDCs; the remaining 40% is due to rural–urban migration. Some of the fastest growing cities are in China. Cities such as Chongqing and Shenzhen grew by more than 10% every year between 2000 and 2005.

Many rural areas, both in the developed and less developed world, have experienced the opposite phenomenon — **depopulation** or an absolute decline in population. Depopulation is caused by net out-migration and ageing rural populations with low birth rates and high death rates.

> **Urbanisation** is an increase in the proportion of a population living in towns and cities.

The impact of change

Revised

Urban areas

Rapid population growth in urban areas in LEDCs often results in overcrowding, inadequate housing, poor services and unemployment. Rates of population growth simply outstrip the resources of urban authorities to cater for increasing numbers. In Nairobi (Kenya) population is currently growing by 200,000 every year and 60% of the city's inhabitants live in **slum settlements** on just 5% of the city's land area. Population densities in the Kibera slum exceed 300,000 persons/km^2 and overcrowding contributes to ill-health and the spread of infectious diseases such as tuberculosis. These settlements are often illegal, unplanned and insanitary. Houses comprise flimsy shacks made of wood, brick, mud, corrugated iron and other rudimentary materials and lack essential services such as mains water supply, sewerage, drainage and electricity. Many squatters are tenants who pay rent to slum landlords. In Kibera slum rents account for 15% of average household incomes and contribute to poverty.

Rural areas

In the UK, long-term net migrational losses often lead to depopulation in rural communities. Some remote regions, such as the northwest highlands and islands of Scotland, and central Wales, have suffered depopulation for decades. Lack of services and limited employment opportunities provide the impetus

> **Examiner's tip**
>
> It is important to distinguish between urbanisation and urban growth. Urbanisation means an increase in the *proportion* of urban dwellers in a country or region; urban growth simply refers to an *absolute* increase in the urban population. If rural population growth exceeds urban growth it is possible for urban growth to occur without urbanisation.

for out-migration. Meanwhile in lowland regions, declining employment in agriculture has been the driver of rural depopulation. For example, employment in agriculture fell by 70% in Norfolk between 1950 and 1980.

Natural decrease also plays a part in rural depopulation. Most out-migrants are young adults, which reduces future birth rates and increases the average age of the population. Ageing populations mean fewer births and more deaths, increasing the likelihood of natural decrease and depopulation. Rural depopulation undermines **thresholds** and triggers the decline of transport, retailing, educational and medical services in many parts of rural Britain (Figure 5.5).

> **Threshold** is the minimum number of people or level of spending needed to support a good or service profitably.

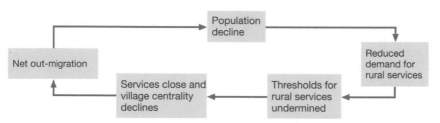

Figure 5.5 Rural depopulation and rural service provision: the vicious circle of decline

Many accessible rural areas in the UK within commuting distance of large urban centres (e.g. Buckinghamshire, Cheshire) have experienced population growth in the past 40 years. This process, known as **counterurbanisation**, is due to urban–rural migration. The impact is felt in several ways:

> **Counterurbanisation** is an increase in the proportion of a population living in rural areas.

- new housing estates encroach on the countryside, and barns and other rural buildings are converted to private dwellings
- soaring house prices, making rural housing unaffordable for local people
- the loss of essential services such general stores, post offices and public transport, which are rarely used by in-comers
- social divisions between in-comers and long-established residents and a loss of community

Inner-city and suburban areas in MEDCs

In developed countries, urban change has given rise to social and economic issues that affect residents in the inner city and in the suburbs. In British cities sharp contrasts in housing, ethnicity, age structure, income and social welfare exist between these two areas.

Inner city
Revised

The inner city is a zone of mixed land use, comprising low-quality housing (late nineteenth/early twentieth-century terraces, 1960s/1970s flats and more recent infill), industry and commerce located within 1 or 2 km of the city centre. Inner-city populations are often poorly qualified, with low incomes and high rates of youth unemployment. Ethnic minorities, attracted by low-cost housing and cultural preferences, are disproportionately represented in inner-city areas. Large concentrations of ethnic groups such as those in Brick Lane in London and Manningham

> **Typical mistake**
>
> The terms 'ghetto' and 'slum' are not synonymous. Slums are neighbourhoods of low-quality housing and inadequate physical infrastructure; ghettos are neighbourhoods dominated by particular ethnic and/or socio-economic groups.

in Bradford form **ghettos**, where residents often lead separate lives from the host society. Social and economic issues in British inner cities focus on **inequality**, **multiple deprivation** and **social exclusion**.

Suburbs

Revised

The suburbs of most British cities grew rapidly during the inter-war and post-war years. Growth was initially driven by improvements in public transport (e.g. trams, suburban trains, bus services) and later by private car ownership. In contrast to the inner city, suburban housing was lower density — typically detached and semi-detached dwellings with gardens. Open areas such as playing fields and parks studded the suburbs, adding to the feeling of space.

Social, economic and demographic changes have created problems in the suburbs. Many local authority estates suffer worse deprivation than inner-city neighbourhoods. Unemployment, ill-health, poor schools, low skill levels and crime are often endemic. A lack of shops selling fresh food contributes to poor diets and ill-health. Unlike inner-city areas, local authority estates are occupied almost exclusively by low-income white communities (e.g. Pennywell in Sunderland, Blackbird Leys in Oxford, Bransholme in Hull). Social dysfunction has been amplified as more aspirational residents have moved out to become owner-occupiers and as local authorities have housed 'problem' families on these estates.

In the outer suburbs, where the built area meets the countryside, there are problems of **urban sprawl**. The problem is likely to get worse. Natural population growth, immigration and the increase in single-person households in the UK mean that the demand for new homes is forecast to grow by nearly 225,000 a year until the mid-2020s. Demand is particularly high in England and in the southeast region, where 654,000 new homes are planned by 2026. Government targets are that at least 60% of new homes should be built on previously developed (**brownfield**) land. This puts huge pressure on **green belt** land, raising issues of loss of countryside and amenity, and the sustainability of urban growth.

> ### Examiner's tip
>
> The image of the inner city in the UK as an area of late nineteenth- and early twentieth-century poor-quality housing and multiple deprivation is too simplistic. Massive urban redevelopment has occurred in many inner cities in the past 50 years. Meanwhile the inner city has proved an increasingly attractive residential location for higher income groups (i.e. gentrification), attracted by access to employment and leisure services in city centres.

> ### Typical mistake
>
> The inner city is often mistakenly thought to include the commercial city centre or CBD. In fact, the inner city is that zone of urban development that lies between the CBD and the suburbs.

Case study — Harehills — inner-city deprivation and decay

Background Harehills is an inner-city suburb in east Leeds. Situated 1–2 km from the city centre, the suburb grew between 1870 and 1914. Much of the original housing (back-to-back terraces) survives today. Two-thirds of the housing is rented from the council, social landlords, and private landlords. Low-cost housing has attracted low-income groups, especially Afro-Caribbean and south Asian ethnic minorities. One-quarter of the ward's population was born outside the UK. The population is relatively youthful, with 28% of residents aged 0–15 years.

Social and economic inequality Harehills is among the poorest 5% of wards in England and a large proportion of its residents suffer multiple deprivation.

According to government assessment, the quality of life in Harehills is 'poor'. Unemployment is twice the Leeds average and is related to poor levels of education and skills. 45% of the adult population have no qualifications and household incomes are less than half those of the prosperous suburban wards. Life expectancy is 4 years below the average for Leeds, and at the 2001 census 12% of residents reported poor health. Substandard housing and overcrowding also contribute to poor health. Reported crime is four times the average for Leeds, with high levels of domestic burglary, vehicle crime and criminal damage. Nearly half of all households qualify for council welfare benefits.

Case study Adel and Wharfedale — suburban prosperity

Background Adel and Wharfedale is a prosperous suburb, dominated by low-density, high-quality detached and semi-detached housing in north Leeds. High property prices and a lack of social and affordable housing excludes lower income groups. Positive externalities include an attractive physical environment on the edge of the city, adjacent to open countryside. The age structure of the population is older than inner-city Harehills with less than 19% of residents aged 15 years or less. Ethnically 95% of the population is white.

Social and economic inequality Adel and Wharfedale ward is barely 4 km from Harehills. Yet inequalities between the residents of the two wards, in terms of life chances, wealth and wellbeing are extreme.

In Harehills, every census super output area (SOA) is in the bottom 10% of SOAs in England. In Adel and Wharfedale the number is zero. Unemployment in Adel and Wharfedale is the lowest in Leeds while in Harehills unemployment is six times higher. Youth unemployment is closely related to qualifications. 82% of school leavers in Adel and Wharfedale have five good GCSEs, compared with 41% in Harehills.

Crime rates are less than one-third of those in Harehills and the suburb has some of the city's most successful state schools.

Now test yourself

11 Describe three adverse effects of rapid urban growth in LEDCs.

12 List three ways in which counterurbanisation creates problems for residents in rural areas in MEDCs.

13 How does rural depopulation affect service provision in rural areas in MEDCs?

14 Suggest three reasons for the segregation of ethnic minority groups in inner city areas in the UK.

15 What is 'multiple deprivation'?

16 How does multiple deprivation link to economic and social exclusion?

Answers on p. 123

Check your understanding

1 Describe the contrasting ways that governments attempt to manage population change.

2 What are the social and economic implications of an ageing population?

3 Describe the social and environmental effects of rapid population growth in cities in LEDCs.

4 What is 'rural depopulation' and what are its implications for rural areas in MEDCs?

Answers on p. 124

Exam practice

1 (a) Study Figure 5.1 which shows the demographic transition model. Describe the pattern of demographic change in Figure 5.1. [4]

(b) Consider the validity and applicability of the demographic transition model for countries at different stages of development. [5]

(c) Outline the impact of population structure on countries at different stages of the demographic transition. [6]

(d) With reference to specific case studies, discuss the attempts made by governments to manage population change. [15]

2 (a) Study Figure 5.4 which shows the pattern of international immigration to the UK between 1990 and 2007. Describe the pattern of migration shown in Figure 5.4. [4]

(b) Suggest reasons for the pattern shown in Figure 5.4. [4]

(c) Describe the economic, social and environmental impact of migration to urban areas in LEDCs. [7]

(d) For an inner-city area and a suburban area, describe and explain the inequalities in social and economic welfare. [15]

Answers and quick quiz 5 online

Online

Examiner's summary

✔ There are several indicators of population change, fertility and mortality. A critical awareness of the value and weaknesses of these indicators (especially vital rates) is important.

✔ The demographic transition model (DTM) provides an understanding of the processes of economic and demographic change. However, its relevance to economic and demographic trends in the developing world today should be questioned.

✔ Unbalanced population structures raise issues of dependency in both MEDCs and LEDCs. Relatively few countries have population structures that approach the optimal.

✔ Remember that 'optimum population' is a relative concept which must be viewed critically. It may refer to a range of economic, technological or environmental criteria. Moreover, there is no unequivocal definition of what constitutes an 'optimum population'.

✔ Migration is both age and sex selective. As a result it is a major influence on population structure at national, regional and local scales.

✔ Net migration is a major driver of population change at national, regional and local scales.

✔ Governments often seek to influence population structure for economic and political reasons. These policies, which usually focus on fertility rates and immigration, often raise controversial issues.

✔ Don't conflate urbanisation and urban growth. Although they are often found together, urban growth can occur in the absence of urbanisation.

✔ Urbanisation, counterurbanisation and depopulation are current trends that have economic, demographic, social and environmental effects in both urban and rural areas. These effects are often controversial.

✔ Inequality within cities in MEDCs is exemplified by the economic, social and demographic contrasts between the inner city and the suburbs. Inequality is most evident in intra-urban contrasts in deprivation (e.g. in education, work and health) and human wellbeing.

✔ You should appreciate that change is an inevitable and ongoing feature of cities. Few urban areas have undergone more transformation in cities in the UK (and elsewhere in the economically developed world) than inner cities.

6 Food supply issues

Global food supply, consumption, trade

Global food supply Revised

Food production through crop cultivation and livestock farming is a leading economic activity in most countries. The scale of production depends on the level of demand (both domestic and foreign markets), growing conditions (soil, temperature, rainfall), technology and opportunities for trade.

According to the UN, Asia (excluding the Middle East) accounts for around 45% of the total global food production (by tonnage). In part this reflects Asia's huge internal demand: in 2010, 56% of the world's population lived in Asia. Within Asia, food production is dominated by the world's two most populous countries — China and India. China is home to one-fifth of the world's population and is responsible for a similar proportion of global food output (Figure 6.1). India, with 17% of the global population produces 13% of world food. Globally, China and India also rank first and second, respectively, in the production of the world's two leading food crops — wheat and rice.

In contrast, Africa, with 15% of the global population, accounts for just 8% of world food production. A range of factors limit food production in Africa (especially in sub-Saharan Africa) including droughts, floods, political instability and poverty.

Large-scale food production also occurs in countries with favourable physical environments, extensive areas of farmland and advanced technologies. Thus, countries such as the USA, Canada, Brazil, Argentina and Australia are major food producers.

> **Examiner's tip**
>
> You need to differentiate between: total food production in a country, measured in tonnes or value; the average amount of food produced per person in a country; and the output of food per hectare of cultivated land. The last is a measure of the intensity of production.

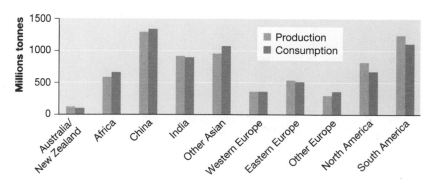

Figure 6.1 Food production and consumption in 2008

Global food consumption and trade Revised

Most food is consumed close to where it is produced and therefore does not enter international trade. Thus, regions and countries with the largest populations, such as China, India, southeast Asia and western Europe, are major food-consuming areas (Figure 6.1). International trade in food generally occurs between areas of food surplus and food deficit. Many countries in North America (USA, Canada) and South America (Brazil, Argentina) have large food surpluses and are significant food exporters. North American food exports exceeded imports by 140 million tonnes in 2008. In the same year South America had a similar export surplus. Australia and New Zealand are also important food exporters, though on a smaller scale.

Food exports flow to areas of food deficit, such as Europe, with its densely populated and highly urbanised regions; Africa, where food shortages go hand-in-hand with poverty; and Asia (including China), with its huge populations and massive demand.

> **Examiner's tip**
>
> In Africa food shortages often result in malnutrition and undernutrition. In MEDCs, overnutrition, leading to obesity, is a major health issue.

The geopolitics of food ······························ Revised ☐

At a global scale, food is increasingly a political issue. In recent years, rising food prices have threatened food scarcity and **food security**. Rising prices are due to a number of factors that affect food production and consumption:

- the global population, increasing by 70 million a year, has increased demand
- the growing wealth of countries such as China drives up demand for meat and dairy products which are grain-intensive
- arable land in North America is being used to grow crops that yield biofuels (e.g. ethanol) rather than food
- climate change, and increased frequencies of droughts and floods reducing food production
- soil erosion and water shortages (e.g. excessive irrigation) due to unsustainable farming
- trade associations between food producers (e.g. Organisation of Rice Exporting Countries) that form cartels that limit production and raise prices

> **Food security** exists when people have adequate physical, social or economic access to food.

Some countries, heavily reliant on food imports and fearing a food crisis, have responded by securing bilateral trade agreements with countries that have surplus farmland. For example, Libya, which imports 90% of its grain, has leased 100,000 ha of farmland in the Ukraine in return for oil exports.

International trade in food is strongly influenced by regional **trade blocs** such as the EU and NAFTA. Trade blocs promote the interests of member states by:

- encouraging free trade between them (e.g. by removing or reducing import duties)
- protecting industries such as agriculture from foreign imports by using tariffs and quotas
- promoting exports such as grain and dairy products by subsidies given to producers

The EU is the largest and most integrated of the regional trade blocs. Within the EU agricultural products and other goods (as well as services, capital and people) move freely. However, most foreign food importers have to pay an import tariff. In addition, farming is heavily subsidised as part of the Common Agricultural Policy, making EU farm products more competitive in foreign markets. This practice is controversial. Foreign governments complain of unfair competition which invariably hits poor farmers in LEDCs hardest.

Agricultural food production systems

Agricultural food production systems are farming enterprises. They have both economic and biological characteristics. A basic agricultural system comprises a group of objects (e.g. farm buildings, machinery, land area) linked by a series of inputs (e.g. labour, capital, seed, fertiliser, water) and outputs (e.g. crops, livestock, wastes). Farming systems can be identified according to their:

- commercial/non-commercial characteristics
- intensity of production
- types of enterprise (i.e. crops, livestock)

Commercial and non-commercial farming
Revised

In **commercial farming** systems, crops and livestock products are exchanged for cash. Most production leaves farms and is sold to markets which include lengthy supply chains of food wholesalers, food manufacturers and supermarkets. Farming systems in MEDCs, ranging from giant agribusiness enterprises to small farmers, are exclusively commercial. In LEDCs commercial farming dominates the agricultural export sector, though most peasant farmers exchange part of their production in local markets for cash. Commercial farming usually relies on large-scale investment in plant and machinery.

Non-commercial or **subsistence farming** is a system where crops and livestock products remain on the farm or smallholding. Production is primarily for the consumption of farmers and their families. Food supply chains are short and production is based on low technology.

Intensive and extensive farming
Revised

Farming intensity describes the output of crops or livestock products, measured in tonnage or value, per hectare or per km^2 of farmland. High-intensity systems that produce high outputs per hectare depend on high inputs of labour, technology, fertiliser etc. Farm systems that rely on large labour inputs to produce high yields per hectare are said to be **labour intensive**. Labour-intensive systems, such as wet rice cultivation in southeast Asia, give high yields per hectare but relatively low yields per person.

Farming systems that use large amounts of capital per hectare (e.g. machinery, chemical fertiliser, pesticides) are said to be **capital intensive**. Overall yields per hectare in capital-intensive systems are often low, though yields per person are high. Systems with a low yield per area cultivated are known as **extensive** farming systems. They include grain cultivation in countries such as Canada and Australia. However, capital-intensive farming can also give high yields per hectare. Examples include cereal farming in eastern England and horticulture in the Netherlands.

> **Examiner's tip**
>
> Think of intensive farming as a high input–high output production system.

> **Typical mistake**
>
> Farm systems in LEDCs are not wholly subsistence-based. Most combine subsistence crops with enterprises geared to the production that is sold for cash.

Types of farming enterprise in MEDCs
Revised

Arable

Arable farming produces food crops such as wheat, barley, oilseed, sugar beet and so on. In Europe, arable farming often occupies high-quality farmland where climate, soil and relief favour cultivation. In these circumstances arable farming often enjoys a **comparative advantage** over alternative enterprises. Throughout the developed world, arable farming is capital intensive, using heavy machinery such as tractors, combine harvesters and grain driers. Yields are high because of large inputs of agro-chemicals.

Livestock

Livestock enterprises range from dairy farming and cattle rearing to intensive battery hen and egg production. Free-range cattle and sheep farming often dominate regions of excessive or deficient rainfall, and/or where soils and relief are unfavourable to cultivation. The artificial environments created for intensive pig and poultry farming make these enterprises relatively **footloose** in location.

Mixed

Mixed farming enterprises combine both arable and livestock production. This type of farming has become less popular as it limits the scope for **scale economies** associated with specialisms such as arable or livestock. However, where physical conditions permit, mixed farming may flourish as a means of supplying large livestock populations with grain and other animal feeds grown on the farm.

> **Comparative advantage** describes how a farming enterprise will specialise in those crops it can grow most efficiently because of favourable physical and economic conditions.

Now test yourself

1 Name the main regions of food deficit and food surplus.
2 State three factors that influence the scale of food production within a country.
3 Give three reasons why world food prices have increased in recent years.
4 State three ways in which international trade blocs influence the global trade in food.
5 Draw a diagram to show a farming enterprise as a system.
6 What distinguishes commercial farming systems from subsistence systems?
7 Give examples of intensive and extensive farming systems.

Answers on p. 124

Managing food supply

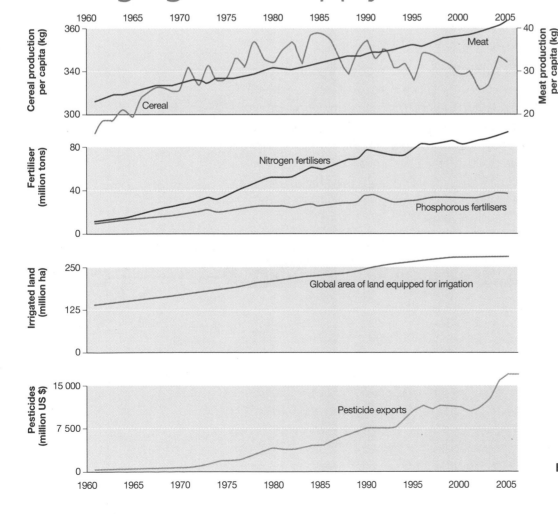

Figure 6.2 Global trends in food supply

Food supplies can be managed by increasing production (Figure 6.2). Strategies used to raise production include the application of new and intermediate technologies, land colonisation, land reform and commercialisation.

High technology 'fixes' — Revised

The Green Revolution

The **Green Revolution** of the 1960s and 1970s centred on a package of new **high-yielding varieties** (HYVs) of rice and wheat, irrigation and chemical fertilisers. Its primary objective was to increase crop yields in the developing world by intensification, and therefore food supplies. The Green Revolution was widely adopted in Asia. There food production increased substantially (e.g. India's output of padi rice grew from 53.5 million tonnes in 1961 to 80.3 million tonnes in 1980).

Despite successfully increasing total food supply, the Green Revolution had a variable impact. Higher income groups in rural societies, with access to irrigation and the resources to purchase chemical fertilisers, gained most. Also, because HYVs had little immunity to disease, farmers only benefited from the new crops if they had the resources to buy expensive pesticides. Not surprisingly, the poorest groups (landless families, general labourers, small-scale farmers) derived few advantages. As a result the Green Revolution tended to increase inequalities in rural societies and did little to improve food security for the poor.

The Green Revolution also often had a negative effect on women in rural societies. The need for cash income to pay for fertilisers and pesticides forced many women to work as agricultural labourers. This process forced down rural wages, leaving millions of women with insufficient income to improve their diets.

> **Examiner's tip**
>
> Be aware that relatively high-tech approaches to increasing production in LEDCs (such as the Green Revolution) may generate inequality, with few benefits for the majority of farmers.

Genetically modified crops

The HYVs of the Green Revolution were produced by selective plant breeding for bigger and better crops. Genetic modification (GM) takes selective breeding a stage further by transplanting desirable genes from one plant into another. GM has enormous potential to solve the world's food shortages, but it is highly controversial, mainly because of its unknown impact on the environment in the long term. By 2009, after 13 years of use, only 25 countries had adopted some GM crops. Currently, seven EU countries grow GM crops but they occupy only 108,000 ha of farmland out of the 60 million ha available in the EU. The only GM crop grown in the EU in 2009 was insect-resistant maize.

Creating new farmland; reorganising existing farmland — Revised

Land colonisation

Food production can be increased by taking more land into cultivation. Often government-inspired, this approach usually means clearing tropical forest for agriculture and encouraging new farmers to settle. In the 1960s, 1970s and 1980s, land colonisation in Brazil's Amazon rainforest was promoted by the government in order to tap the region's agricultural and other natural resources. Tens of thousands of families, driven by poverty, flooded into Amazonian states such as Rondônia, Acre and Pará. The government gave subsistence farmers 100 ha plots of forest, a few basic tools and seeds. Other subsistence farmers squatted on forest land, gaining automatic legal title after 5 years of occupancy. However, the impoverished forest soils made subsistence farming unsustainable. The majority of farmers abandoned their plots after a few years and sold them to commercial cattle ranchers. Today, around 75% of deforested land in the Brazilian Amazon is used for commercial ranching. Although rates of deforestation have fallen dramatically since the 1980s, nearly 7,500 km^2 of forest was cleared in 2009, 60% of this in Pará state.

Land reform

Land reform is government-organised redistribution of agricultural land. The motives for land reform are usually economic and political (e.g. social justice). In economic terms land reform improves farm efficiency and the intensity of production and output by enlarging or consolidating farm plots, and increasing motivation and innovation among farmers who become owner-occupiers or secure tenants.

Taiwan implemented a successful land reform programme in the early 1950s. Before reform, Taiwan was a nation of **sharecroppers**. Most land was owned by just 20 families; average farms were barely 1 ha in size; and farm rents were 50–70% of the value of crop production. Land reform included:

- massive rent reductions, and longer leases to tenants
- government-owned land sold to farmers at below market prices
- easy credit terms to farmers wanting to buy their own land
- large landowners forced to sell most of their land and compensated by the government

> **Sharecroppers** are tenant farmers whose rent is a proportion of annual farm production.

The results were dramatic. Over 400,000 farming families became owner-occupiers and tenancy rates dropped from 64% to 17%. Farm production increased at an annual rate of 5.6% between 1953 and 1970. For the first time, farmers had the incentive to use more fertiliser and introduce multicropping, growing up to four crops a year. In addition many farmers innovated by diversifying into higher value, more intensive horticultural crops.

Market economies and intermediate technologies

Revised

Commercialisation

The **commercialisation** of agriculture describes the move from subsistence farming to greater involvement with the market. The process usually applies to small family farms in the developing world. With commercialisation, production becomes increasingly oriented towards **cash crops**, sold in regional, national and export markets. Meanwhile farmers rely on the market for vital inputs such as fertilisers, pesticides, credit and advisory services.

> **Examiner's tip**
>
> Commercialisation of farming remains controversial. Commercialisation may: increase rural inequality, make it difficult for small farmers to compete, expose farmers to foreign producers, and force some farmers to abandon agriculture.

Although commercialisation does not benefit all farmers, and may increase rural inequality, connection to the **market economy** raises productivity and farm incomes. Farming becomes more efficient and more specialised, while **food security**, including food affordability, nutritive value and availability, improves.

Intermediate technology

Intermediate technology in agriculture, such as irrigation from boreholes and wells, and the introduction of simple soil and **water** conservation techniques can boost food production and farm incomes, and improve the nutrition and health of farming families. Improvements of this kind, based on simple technologies, have a number of advantages:

- they often rely on local resources
- they are low-cost and easy to implement and maintain
- in the long-term they are economically and environmentally sustainable

Development programmes that rely on intermediate technology are widespread in countries in sub-Saharan Africa and throughout the developing world. They are often supported by non-governmental organisations (**NGOs**) such as Oxfam and Water Aid, and are usually small scale, targeting villages and rural districts. Examples include: drilling wells or boreholes to provide water for irrigation and tackle problems of water shortages during the dry season, reafforestation to prevent soil erosion and fencing-off pasture lands to stop overgrazing by livestock.

> **Now test yourself**
>
> 8 What is the Green Revolution?
> 9 Make a table listing the advantages and disadvantages of the Green Revolution.
> 10 Why are GM crops controversial?
> 11 Why was land colonisation often unsuccessful in Amazonia?
> 12 What is the commercialisation of agriculture?
> 13 List the advantages of the application of intermediate technology in farming.
>
> Answers on p. 124

Managing food supply in the EU

The Common Agricultural Policy   Revised ☐

Food production in the EU and international trade in food between the EU and its trading partners is controlled by the EU's Common Agricultural Policy (CAP). The aims of the CAP are to:

- increase agricultural productivity
- ensure a fair standard of living for the agricultural community
- stablise market prices for food
- secure food supplies
- provide consumers with food at reasonable prices

The CAP has two major components or 'pillars'.

- Pillar 1 gives financial support and protection to farmers
- Pillar 2 supports the broader responsibilities of agriculture in terms of environmental protection and developing rural economies

Pillar 1: strategies to influence food production

The CAP provides financial support to farmers through direct cash payments, intervention prices, export subsidies and import tariffs (Table 6.1). Direct single payments are subject to farmers satisfying **cross-compliance** regulations (e.g. conservation of habitats and wildlife, food hygiene, animal welfare etc.).

Table 6.1 EU Common Agricultural Policies

Direct Single Payments	Since 2003 farmers have received single payments for crops and livestock. Payments are based on hectarage farmed, not production. Single payments have helped to prevent overproduction. Milk quotas (due to be phased out in 2015) have a similar purpose.
Intervention prices	A minimal intervention price for each crop is agreed annually by the EU. If market prices fall below the intervention price the EU buys the goods to raise the price to the intervention level.
Subsidies	Some EU crops are subsidised by the CAP. Subsidies are controversial because they give EU farmers an unfair advantage in foreign markets. It is hoped to phase out all export subsidies by 2013.
Import tariff	The EU is a customs union and food imports incur a common tariff. The average tariff is around 16%.

Pillar 2: environmental protection

Farming has a huge influence on rural landscapes, ecosystems and rural economies. Its importance in this context is recognised by the EU, forming the second pillar of the CAP. In the environmental sphere, farmers only qualify for financial support if they meet minimal environmental standards. This policy is known as cross-compliance. It includes:

- limits on stocking levels for sheep in the uplands
- limits on the use of chemical fertiliser
- reduced inputs of pesticides
- leaving strips of uncultivated land around fields to create wildlife habitats
- taking steps to reduce soil erosion

Table 6.2 gives a summary of the main agri-environmental schemes available to farmers in the UK.

Table 6.2 Agri-environmental schemes available in the UK

Set-aside	The EU policy of **set-aside** was introduced in 1992. Its primary aim was to reduce overproduction of food by taking arable land out of cultivation. Farmers were compensated financially for loss of production. Set-aside had important benefits for wildlife: unploughed fields provide cover, habitats, food and nesting sites for birds. Following world grain shortages, the EU abolished set-aside in 2008.
Environmentally Sensitive Areas (ESAs)	A UK initiative, launched in 1987, the ESA scheme focused on environmental protection through farm management. Farmers who entered the scheme and farmed in an environmentally sensitive way were compensated for lost production, e.g. £70/ha for rough pasture, £150/ha for traditional hay meadows. The ESA scheme covered nearly 6,000 km^2 of countryside of high environmental value and was highly successful. Now closed, it has been replaced by the Environmental Stewardship scheme.
Environmental Stewardship (ES)	ES was introduced by Natural England in 2005. It rewards farmers for conservation and environmental enhancement of the countryside. Farmers receive funding for using methods that conserve wildlife and biodiversity, protect historic environments and natural resources, and maintain and enhance the quality and character of the landscape.

> **Examiner's tip**
>
> Overproduction of food is no longer a problem in the EU. As a result the environment and rural development have much greater prominence in the CAP today.

Changes in demand

High-value food exports from LEDCs
Revised

Rising incomes, advances in transport technology, trade liberalisation and the dominance of large supermarkets in food retailing have driven the growth in demand for high-value agricultural (HVA) products such fresh fruit and vegetables in MEDCs. HVA food exports are simply another facet of **globalisation**. Many small-scale farmers in the developing world have benefited from this growing market. Others, however, unable to meet the standardisation and quality requirements of supermarket chains, fail to reap the advantages of HVA production.

Compared with traditional export crops such as coffee, cocoa and bananas, HVA crops suffer less from price fluctuations in world markets. Today, HVA crops account for half of all agri-food exports by value from LEDCs. This compares with just 30% between 1980 and 1991.

Year-round demand for seasonal foodstuffs

Revised

Around 30 or 40 years ago, most fresh fruit and vegetables were produced locally and their availability was highly seasonal. However, since the 1980s, what were seasonal foods have become available all year round. This has been made possible by air freight linking overseas producers with supermarkets and consumers. Lifestyle changes and lower real prices for out-of-season foods (as a result of bulk-buying by supermarkets and lower air freight costs) have also boosted year-round demand for fresh fruit and vegetables. But this global sourcing of seasonal food raises issues of excessive 'air miles' and carbon emissions that contribute to global warming and climate change.

Organic food products

Revised

Organic farming is the production of food without using **agro-chemicals** such as synthetic fertilisers and pesticides in crop growing, and drugs and antibiotics in livestock farming. Organic produce has become increasingly popular in MEDCs since the 1980s. This trend is consumer-led, and is driven by demands for healthier food and better animal welfare. The major supermarket chains have been quick to respond and sell a wide range of organic fruit, vegetables, meat and dairy products. However, organic food has higher production and distribution costs than non-organic food. As a result it has a price premium which makes it a luxury item. Even so, in the USA organic food accounted for nearly 4% of food sales in 2010 and continues to grow rapidly.

Regional and local food sourcing

Revised

The past 10 years or so have seen an increasing emphasis on the regional and local sourcing of food in MEDCs. This trend is a reaction to the globalisation of food production. In the UK, major supermarkets such as Tesco and Waitrose are keen to promote locally grown produce such as fruit, vegetables, cheese, ice cream, bacon, honey and so on. Traditional markets and farmers markets are also important outlets for locally grown foods. Local food sourcing has a number of advantages:

- small, family-run farms can compete and sell directly to supermarkets
- employment is provided for the local economy
- it is 'greener': supply chains are shortened and with less transport and storage, energy costs, 'food miles' and pollution are reduced

> **Examiner's tip**
>
> Be aware that there are strong arguments on economic and environmental grounds for supporting local food producers, even though this may limit the seasonal availability of some foods.
>
> Organic food production arouses controversy; it is often seen as irrelevant to most consumers in MEDCs who cannot afford the premium prices.

Food supplies in a globalising economy

The role of transnational corporations

Revised

Large international companies or **transnational corporations** (TNCs) dominate all stages of the global food chain, from inputs of fertiliser, pesticide and seed, to farming, food processing and retailing. For instance, half the world's

Exam practice answers and quick quizzes at **www.therevisionbutton.co.uk/myrevisionnotes**

bananas are marketed by just two American TNCs (Chiquita and Dole). Many TNCs involved in the global food chain, such as Coca Cola, Unilever, Monsanto, McDonald's and Wal-Mart, are household names.

In production terms, TNCs are closely connected to **agribusiness**. This type of farming is large scale, capital intensive and uses modern technology and science. Because agribusiness produces food at low cost, it is attractive to TNCs driven by the need to make profits. Food-processing TNCs often contract farmers to grow crops and livestock products, supply farmers with inputs such as seed and fertiliser and even provide loans for farm buildings and machinery. At the same time, they have direct control over which crops farmers grow, their quality, and how they are produced, processed and distributed.

Although some TNCs concentrate on just one stage in the production chain (e.g. a chemical giant such as Bayer producing synthetic fertiliser), others, such as food processors (e.g. McCains) and supermarkets (e.g. Wal-Mart) control several stages of the food chain.

The dominance of TNCs in the global food system raises a number of issues.

- Do contract farmers get a fair return for their products? Value is added at each stage of the food chain, and farmers often receive only a fraction of the price that food manufacturers and retailers charge for food products.
- Does contract farming discriminate against small, family-run farms, unable to provide the bulk production required by TNCs?
- Do TNCs that rely on agribusiness contribute to rural unemployment, out-migration and the decline of rural communities?

> **Examiner's tip**
>
> When discussing geographical issues, you must provide a balanced response. By definition, issues are controversial, with arguments on both sides. As well as adopting and justifying a particular viewpoint you need to counter opposing arguments.

Environmental aspects of the global trade in food

Revised

The global trade in food creates adverse environmental effects at local and global scales.

In many developing countries, agribusiness and the production of crops for export has contributed to **environmental degradation**. The benefits of scale economies and the introduction of new farming techniques often result in crop **monocultures** (e.g. sugar, coffee, bananas) and the intensive use of agro-chemicals. Adverse environmental effects include soil erosion, the **eutrophication** of watercourses and loss of **biodiversity**. In central America, commercial beef production for export has caused widespread deforestation and soil erosion. In Guatemala, American TNCs such as Chiquita, Dole and Del operate vast plantations producing export crops of fruit and vegetables that occupy the best farmlands. As a knock-on effect, native farmers are forced to cultivate steep land in the Western Highlands, which is environmentally unsustainable.

At the global scale, trade in food increases 'food miles'. International food transport (in particular air freighting of perishable crops such as fruit and vegetables) is a major contributor to fossil fuel use, pollution and greenhouse gas emissions. In the UK, the transport of imported food and animal feed is responsible for 4 million tonnes of CO_2 emissions

> **Monoculture** is the large-scale cultivation of a single crop. It exhausts soil fertility and increases the risks of crop disease.
>
> **Eutrophication** is oxygen deficiency in rivers and lakes. Nutrient enrichment by runoff charged with nitrates and phosphates stimulates algal growth. Bacteria feed off the dead algae and deplete oxygen levels in the water, thus destroying aquatic life.

annually. Meanwhile, forest clearance, associated with livestock farming in the tropics and subtropics, contributes significantly to rising levels of greenhouse gases that drive global warming and climate change.

The potential for sustainable food supplies

World food production increased massively in the twentieth century, resulting in a fall in the proportion of the world's population that is undernourished. Yet the absolute number of people suffering undernutrition actually increased to nearly 1 billion. In 2007 global calorie intake per person averaged nearly 2800 kcal/day. However, people in the world's least developed countries averaged just 2,160 kcal/person/day — 23% below the world average. With the global population expected to rise in the next 40 years by a further 2.5 billion (from 6.9 to 9.3 billion), there are real concerns that food supplies will fail to keep pace with population growth, particularly in sub-Saharan Africa.

Food production can be increased in three ways:

- extending the areas of crop and grazing land
- raising yields per hectare (new crop strains, genetic engineering)
- increasing cropping intensity

In recent decades, increases in total food production have mainly come from improved yields because of more irrigation and the greater use of chemical fertilisers and pesticides. The scope for further increases in production by improving yields and extending the cultivated land area is limited. Rather than increasing food production, a more practical and sustainable approach to prevent future food shortages is to (a) reduce food wastage and (b) reduce consumption of meat and other livestock products.

Food wastage

Significant losses of food occur between harvesting crops and their consumption. According to the UN only 43% of cereals produced worldwide are available for consumption. Losses occur during harvest, storage and transport. Similar losses are incurred by fisheries, which account for 10% of total human calorie intake. Of the annual global fish catch of 110–130 million tonnes, 30 million tonnes are discarded. In the EU, the Common Fisheries Policy sets limits (quotas) on the size of catches that can be landed. If fishermen exceed their quotas, the surplus catch is discarded (dead) at sea.

Livestock farming

Greater efficiency in food consumption can be achieved by reducing the proportion of food crops that are fed to livestock. The UN estimates that the non-food use of cereals is sufficient to support an extra 3.5 billion people — enough to feed the global population in 2050 without any increase in production. Diverting grain and other crops to feed livestock is highly inefficient: it requires 3 kg of grain and 16,000 litres of water to produce 1 kg of meat. In 2010, roughly one-third of all arable land was devoted to animal feed.

Examiner's tip

For exam questions on feeding the world's population in the twenty-first century, you should focus on two areas: increasing food supply and reducing demand. Total food production can be increased by raising yields, extending the cultivated area and improving efficiency (e.g. cutting waste). However, sustainability cannot be achieved without a reduction in demand (e.g. population control, changes in diet — fewer meat and dairy products).

Sustainability

The expansion of livestock farming in the twentieth century caused widespread damage to the environment, often in the poorest countries. Vast areas of forest in Latin America have been cleared to provide low-quality grazing land. 70% of grazing land in this region is now degraded because of overgrazing and soil erosion. The environmental impact of deforestation is considerable. Loss of habitat results in a reduction of biodiversity. At a global scale, deforestation is a major contributor to rising levels of greenhouse gases (GHGs) in the atmosphere, while livestock alone account for 18% of annual GHG emissions. A sustainable agriculture is essential, not only to ensure food security but also to maintain healthy ecosystems.

Case study — Food supply and demand in India

Background During the past 40 years the Indian government's priority has been to boost domestic food production to feed its rapidly growing population and ensure national food security. India's population grew from 554 million in 1970 to 1,190 million in 2011 (Figure 6.3).

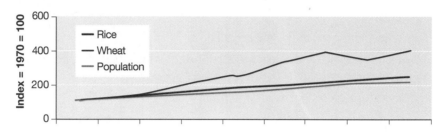

Figure 6.3 India: growth of cereal production and population 1970–2008

Policies and methods Progress in food production was achieved with the introduction of high-yielding varieties of cereals, the widespread use of irrigation and the application of chemical fertiliser — a package of measures known as the Green Revolution.

The government also helped to increase food production by subsidising farm inputs such as power, water and fertiliser and by supporting food prices. A proportion of the wheat and rice crop is purchased by government at support prices (normally less than the market price) and is sold to consumers at subsidised prices. The state also supplies other essential foods such as sugar and edible oil at subsidised prices.

Outcomes During the 1970s and 1980s outputs of staple crops such as rice and wheat increased, and more than kept pace with population growth (Figure 6.3).

Government price subsidies have (a) encouraged production (by giving income stability to farmers), and (b) protected the poorest consumers from food price increases.

Increased food production has reduced rural poverty by creating more jobs. However, although India has achieved self-sufficiency in basic foodstuffs, the poorest one-fifth of the population still experience food insecurity.

Now test yourself

14 Write down the main features of EU strategies for food security and environmental protection.

15 List the arguments for and against high-value crops.

16 What is: (a) organic farming, (b) agribusiness?

17 What are the arguments supporting the sourcing of food locally?

18 Draw a diagram to show the main features of the food chain, from producer to consumer.

19 What are TNCs? Name three TNCs that operate in the food chain.

Answers on p. 124

Check your understanding

1 Describe and explain how geopolitics has influenced food production, consumption and trade.
2 Outline one agricultural food production system and explain how it varies geographically.
3 Evaluate the effectiveness of strategies for increasing food production in LEDCs.
4 How and with what success has the CAP managed food production within the EU?

Answers on p. 125

Exam practice

1 (a) (i) Study Figure 6.1 which shows global patterns of food production and consumption in 2008. Describe the global patterns of food production and consumption in Figure 6.1. [4]

 (ii) Discuss the implications of global patterns of food production and consumption in Figure 6.1 for international trade in food. [5]

 (b) Explain how land reform can influence food supply. [6]

 (c) With reference to case studies, discuss the effectiveness of contrasting approaches to the management of food supply and demand. [15]

2 (a) Describe the Green Revolution in agricultural production. [4]

 (b) Study Figure 6.3 which shows rice and wheat production and population growth in India between 1970 and 2008. Outline and comment on the trends shown in Figure 6.3. [5]

 (c) Outline the arguments for supporting the local/regional sourcing of food. [5]

 (d) Discuss the role of transnational corporations in the production, processing and distribution of food. [15]

Answers and quick quiz 6 online

Online

Examiner's summary

✔ Global food production, consumption and trade are influenced by a range of economic, social, demographic, political and environmental factors.

✔ Remember that food availability has important implications for human health. Food shortages often result in malnutrition and undernutrition, while overnutrition leading to obesity is a major health issue.

✔ Most food is grown for domestic consumption and does not enter international trade (e.g. Africa, China, India).

✔ Global food supplies have kept pace with rising demand in the past 40 years as new technologies have intensified production and new land has been taken into cultivation.

✔ You should be aware that high-tech approaches to increasing production in LEDCs (e.g. the Green Revolution) also have a downside. They may widen the gap between rich and poor, and provide few benefits to the majority of farmers.

✔ Global demand for food will continue to increase as world population continues to grow rapidly and living standards rise. Meeting this demand will be a major challenge in the twenty-first century.

✔ A range of factors influences types of farming enterprise including access to markets, technology, government policies, population pressure, climate and soils. You should be aware of the relative importance of economic, social and physical factors.

✔ The commercialisation of farming does not always benefit small farmers in the less developed world.

✔ Farming in MEDCs is not just about food production but also about managing the countryside.

✔ The globalisation of food production, driven by TNCs and agribusiness, has economic, social and environmental benefits and disbenefits.

✔ Any discussion of geographical issues, such as the commercialisation of farming, requires a balanced approach. By definition, issues are controversial, with arguments on both sides. In addition to justifying your own stance you also need to consider alternative (opposing) views.

✔ The issue of feeding the world's population in the twenty-first century should focus on (a) increasing food supply and (b) reducing demand (e.g. eliminating waste).

7 Energy issues

Types of energy

There are two major categories of energy resources: **non-renewables** (stock) and **renewables** (flow). Non-renewables comprise **fossil fuels** such as coal, oil and natural gas. They take millions of years to form and are therefore finite. Renewables are more diverse and include wind power, hydroelectric power (HEP), solar power, biofuels and several others. Unlike fossil fuels, renewables are either recyclable (e.g. biofuels) or inexhaustible (e.g. solar power). About 80% of total world energy supply in 2011 came from coal, oil and gas; 10% was provided by combustible renewables (mainly wood) — the main source of energy for millions of rural dwellers in the developing world.

Primary and secondary energy
Revised ☐

Primary energy is energy that has not been converted or transformed from its original state. Coal, oil and gas are examples of primary energy. **Secondary energy** is electricity, produced by burning fossil fuels, by nuclear fission, by hydro power and so on.

Energy mix
Revised ☐

Energy mix describes the combination of primary fuels that power a country's economy. Several factors can influence a country's energy mix.

- Domestic sources of primary energy — Energy resources available within a country are often cheaper than imports and also represent a more reliable supply. China and India, with huge coal reserves, have energy economies dominated by this fuel.

- Energy security — A country may opt for a diversified energy mix in order to avoid excessive dependence on just one or two imported fuels. This is important where energy supplies originate in exporting regions that are politically unstable (e.g. oil from the Middle East) or unreliable (e.g. gas from Russia).

- Levels of development — MEDCs rely on primary energy resources such as fossil fuels and nuclear power (Figure 7.1), while many LEDCs continue to use traditional biofuels such as fuelwood, crop residues and animal dung (Figure 7.2).

- Environment — Many rich countries have attempted to move away from the more polluting fossil fuels (especially coal) in favour of natural gas, hydro power and renewables. The aim is to reduce GHG emissions and comply with international obligations on climate change.

> **Examiner's tip**
>
> When explaining the concept of energy mix it is important to use actual examples and give due emphasis to the increasingly prominent role of political and environmental factors.

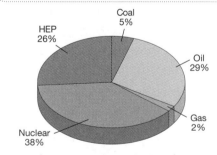

Figure 7.1 Energy mix: Sweden

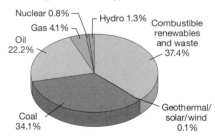

Figure 7.2 Energy mix: India

Global patterns of energy supply, consumption and trade

Coal

In 2009, coal supplied 27% of global primary energy needs. At the global scale coal reserves are widely distributed (Figure 7.3). With the exception of South America, all continents have substantial **reserves**.

> **Reserves** are energy resources that can be developed profitably under current economic conditions and with existing technologies.

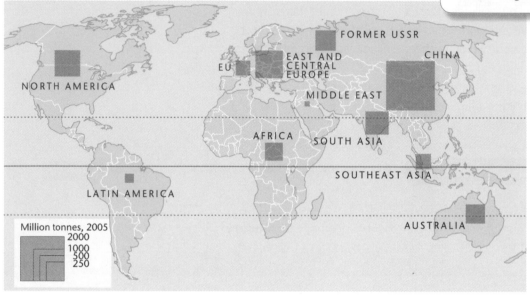

Figure 7.3 World coal production

The top five coal producers are China, the USA, India, Australia and South Africa. They account for nearly 80% of global production. China is by far the largest producer, responsible for 48% of global output in 2009. Global coal reserves were estimated at 825 billion tonnes, which is sufficient to last, at 2009 rates of production, for another 120 years.

Unlike other fossil fuels, less than one-quarter of world coal production enters international trade. Most is consumed domestically in the country of production. This is particularly true of China, India and the USA. The principal coal-exporting countries are Australia, Indonesia and Russia. Coal is less transportable than oil and gas because of:

- its larger proportion of waste
- its lower calorific value
- its solid physical state
- its lack of versatility, i.e. it has limited value for the transport industry

Coal mining depends crucially on production costs. Costs are influenced by geological conditions such as the depth of coal deposits, the thickness of coal seams, the quality of the coal, and the degree of faulting. They are lowest where coal crops out near the surface and can be mined by **open-casting**. In contrast, **deep mining** is more expensive and allows the recovery of little more than half of all reserves. Thanks to cheap open-cast mining and low freight rates, Australia, the world's leading coal exporter, is able to ship coal half way round the world to Europe and still undercut the price of locally produced coal.

> **Examiner's tip**
>
> In response to questions on the exhaustion of fossil fuel reserves, be clear that most estimates of reserves are only approximate, that many potential reserves lie undiscovered, and that reserves fluctuate according to world prices and levels of demand. Thus, reserve estimates should be treated with some scepticism.

Oil Revised

Oil is the leading fossil fuel. World production in 2009 was 3.82 billion tonnes. Its geography of production is highly concentrated, with 70% of global output originating in the Middle East, the OECD countries (mainly the USA) and the former USSR (Table 7.1). Of global proven oil reserves, 57% are located in the Middle East.

Two of the world's largest oil producers — the USA and China — cannot satisfy domestic demand from their own resources, and rely on oil imports. Other major oil importers such as the EU and Japan have minimal resources of their own. Oil exports are dominated by the Middle East, especially Saudi Arabia, Iran, Iraq, the UAE and Kuwait (Table 7.1). Between them, these five countries accounted for 43% of world oil exports in 2009. Russia, Nigeria, Norway, Mexico and Venezuela are also important oil exporters. Because crude oil is shipped in huge tankers, transport costs per tonne/km are low and distance from markets has little influence on production. For example, the typical cost of transporting crude oil from the Middle East to the USA works out at only 0.5 cents per litre. Around one-half of annual global oil production enters international trade.

Table 7.1 Leading oil producers, 2009

Country	Oil production (millions tonnes)
Russia	494
Saudi Arabia	460
USA	325
Iran	202
China	189
Canada	156
Mexico	148
Venezuela	125
Iraq	122
UAE	121

Natural gas Revised

Natural gas accounts for one-fifth of global primary energy production. At the global scale, production is widely dispersed. In the past 30 years natural gas production has increased more rapidly than either oil or coal. This is partly because:

- gas reserves are large (especially in Russia and the Middle East)
- gas is easier to transport and store (by pipeline and as liquid natural gas)
- gas is a cleaner and more environmentally acceptable energy

Natural gas is complex to handle and requires large investment in pipelines, **liquefied natural gas** (LNG) carriers and storage facilities. In addition, many gas resources such as those in Siberia and North Africa are distant from consuming centres. As a result only around one-quarter of gas production is traded internationally. Of this, 21% is in the form of LNG. The construction and management of international pipelines in remote or environmentally sensitive areas presents major logistical problems. Pipelines are also vulnerable to war and sabotage in regions of political instability such as the Middle East.

Recent changes Revised

The main trend in global primary energy use has been the almost uninterrupted growth in production and consumption of the past 30 years. During this period production and consumption of coal has doubled, oil has increased one and a half times, and natural gas has grown threefold. The spectacular rise in coal production and consumption is mainly due to China, where production grew from 600 million tonnes in

1980 to over 3,000 million tonnes in 2009. Despite this, demand is so high in China that the country is also a significant coal importer (mainly coking coal from Australia).

Recent increases in global oil production have been less spectacular, but nonetheless rapid. While production and exports from Middle East countries have been fairly stable since 1980, Russia, West Africa and South and Central America have become major exporters. At the same time demand for oil has remained static in Europe, has doubled in the USA and has increased sharply in emerging economies such as China and India.

Three-quarters of natural gas exports are distributed by pipeline, the remainder in LNG form by sea. The EU and eastern Europe have become increasingly dependent on gas delivered by pipeline from Russia. The UK supplements its own gas supplies with large imports by pipeline from Norway's North Sea gasfields. Piped gas is also transferred in large volumes from Canada to the USA. LNG exports have grown conspicuously in countries poorly connected to international gas pipeline networks, such as Japan, South Korea and Spain. Qatar, Australia, Algeria and Malaysia are major exporters of LNG.

> **Now test yourself**
>
> 1 Make lists of the following types of energy resources: renewables, non-renewables, recyclable, inexhaustible.
> 2 State two disadvantages of fossil fuels.
> 3 What is the difference between primary and secondary energy?
> 4 Which countries are the major producers and consumers of coal, oil and gas?
> 5 What have been the main trends in global energy patterns in the past 30 years?
>
> Answers on p. 125

The geopolitics of energy

Fossil fuels drive the global economy. Because of their importance, political factors play a prominent part in the production, consumption and trade in fossil fuels, especially oil.

Energy supplies — Revised ☐

Cartels

Many of the world's biggest oil producers belong to a powerful group known as the Organization of the Petroleum Exporting Countries (OPEC). OPEC is the cartel representing the major oil exporting countries. Its 13 member states produce around 40% of the world's oil and hold around 80% of proven oil reserves. By controlling production, OPEC regulates the amount of oil entering international trade and exerts a powerful influence on oil prices.

International conflict and energy security

Oil prices reflect (a) the international market's confidence in supply, and (b) levels of demand. Despite the influence of OPEC, oil prices are extremely volatile. In 2008 they peaked at US$131/barrel, before falling back to US$39/barrel by the end of the year. However, early in 2011 prices had once again risen to over US$100/barrel. While energy demand is mainly affected by economic factors (e.g. decline in demand during the Great Recession 2008–2009), geopolitical factors have an important influence on energy supply.

Over half of the world's oil reserves are found in the Middle East. Highly unstable, this region has been plunged into political turmoil on numerous occasions in the recent past by war and revolution (e.g. 1973 Israel–Arab war, 2003 Iraq war). Such events threaten production and cause a spike in oil prices. Moreover, some Middle East countries, hostile towards the west, have deliberately cut off supplies in the past.

Though less important to global energy trade, natural gas supplies are also vulnerable to political conflict. In January 2009 a dispute between Russia and Ukraine resulted in Gazprom, the Russian gas supplier, unilaterally shutting off supplies (by pipeline) to Ukraine, which in turn led to gas shortages in Germany and other EU countries.

Energy TNCs

Energy TNCs such as BP and Shell are major players in the global energy system. Four of the ten largest TNCs are oil companies (BP, Exxon, Shell, Total). These corporations have enormous power to influence governments and their energy policies. For example, the decision by the US government to allow drilling for oil in Alaska's Arctic National Wildlife Refuge was influenced by donations by the oil industry to the Republican-controlled Senate and the president. Furthermore, prior to 2009, the US government's longstanding denial of any link between global climate change and burning fossil fuels was influenced by the oil and coal lobby in the USA.

> **Examiner's tip**
>
> Oil is crucial to the world economy, and powerful countries such as the USA, Japan, China and Germany rely heavily on oil imports. Thus major oil-producing areas have great geopolitical significance — a point that should be stressed in any answer on the geopolitics of oil.

Geopolitics and international energy transport

Revised

Oil, and to a lesser extent gas, enter international trade by ocean-going tankers and pipelines. Both tankers and pipelines are vulnerable targets for terrorists, warring factions and pirates. Several major shipping lanes pass through narrow channels or **chokepoints** close to politically unstable areas, such as the Straits of Hormuz (Persian Gulf) and Malacca (Malaysia). In recent years a dozen or so large oil tankers, with cargoes worth up to US$200 million each, have been seized by Somali pirates. Although the motive is primarily economic, the existence of piracy off the coast of east Africa reflects the political anarchy and civil war that exists in Somalia.

Of the world's oil, 40% flows through pipelines that are even more vulnerable than tankers. Saudi Arabia has 15,000 km of pipeline and Iraq 4,000 km. Most of the network is above ground and easily sabotaged. Because of their length, pipelines are difficult to protect and are therefore soft targets for terrorists.

Saudi Arabia's oil installations are especially vulnerable to terrorist attack. Over half of Saudi Arabia's oil production comes from the Ghawar field, while two-thirds of the county's crude oil is processed in a single refinery at Abqaiq. On the Persian Gulf, Saudi Arabia has just two primary oil export terminals: Ras Tanura and Ras al-Ju'aymah. Its Red Sea oil terminal at Yanbu is connected to Abqaiq by a 1,000 km pipeline. An attack on Abqaiq or Ras Tanura could reduce by half Saudi Arabia's production of oil for at least 6 months, with disastrous economic consequences for the world economy and major importers such as the USA, the EU, Japan and China.

> **Examiner's tip**
>
> Organise answers to questions concerned with the environmental impact of energy production according the severity, geographical scale and permanence of the impacts.

Environmental impact of energy production

Environmental impacts

Revised

Most types of energy production and energy use have some adverse environmental effects. The scale of these effects varies from the local to the global (Table 7.2).

Table 7.2 Environmental impact of types of energy

	Local/regional	Global
Biofuels	Timber is widely used as a fuel in the developing world. Rising demand for farmland and fuelwood has resulted in deforestation, soil erosion and land degradation. Some of the most environmentally damaged areas are in the Sahel, in countries such as Niger, Mali and Burkina Faso.	Deforestation contributes to global warming and climate change. Burning timber releases carbon to the atmosphere, and fewer trees result in less biomass storage of carbon.
Coal	Combustion of coal for domestic use, industry and power generation causes local atmospheric pollution (SO_2, particulates) which impacts on human health. Open-cast mining destroys landscapes and habitats. Deep mining causes land subsidence and spoil heaps from mining waste.	The combustion of coal, oil and gas is a major contributor to rising levels of atmospheric GHGs responsible for climate change. Acid rain, caused by emissions of sulphur through coal burning, damages forests and wildlife, and contributes to respiratory diseases.
Oil	Oil spillages (e.g. Niger Delta, Gulf of Mexico) pollute water bodies and damage fragile ecosystems.	
Gas	Flaring natural gas pollutes the atmosphere and damages human health.	
Nuclear	Accidental leakages of radioactive materials from power stations and reprocessing plants contaminate the environment and food chains and adversely affect human health and wildlife. Contaminated nuclear sites may remain radioactive for hundreds of years.	The problem of safe, long-term storage of radioactive waste (to prevent leakage or sabotage) is a potential threat to the global environment.
HEP	Dam construction floods large areas, destroys forests, and terrestrial and aquatic ecosystems. Modified river flows also impact adversely on aquatic ecosystems.	

Nuclear power and its management

Nuclear power production

Revised

Nuclear power produces 6% of total world energy and 15% of the world's electricity. Most nuclear plants are located in the developed world, reflecting the advanced technology required to build and maintain them and the need to control nuclear weapons' proliferation. Countries such as France and Japan, with limited domestic reserves of fossil fuels, have invested heavily in nuclear power. Together, France, Japan and the USA account for over half of global nuclear power production. Uranium fuels the nuclear energy industry. Like fossil fuels, uranium is a finite resource, although it can be recycled. In contrast to oil, uranium reserves are mainly located in politically stable countries such as Canada, Australia and Namibia. Reserves (3.3 million tonnes) are sufficient to last for several decades.

The management of nuclear power

Revised

Nuclear accidents at Three Mile Island in Pennsylvania in 1979, Chernobyl in 1986 and Fukushima in 2011 exposed the dangers of nuclear energy. Accidents of this magnitude tend to harden public opinion against the industry. Nuclear power has to be managed with greater care than other energy industries because:

- accidents involving nuclear power are potentially catastrophic, with the potential to kill and injure hundreds of thousands of people
- radioactive materials released into the environment may remain toxic for thousands of years, enter food chains and pose long-term health risks to human populations

- no secure repository for radioactive waste and spent uranium fuel has yet been built anywhere in the world
- nuclear installations are potential targets for terrorists and vulnerable to earthquakes, rising sea level and tsunamis

Management of nuclear power focuses on reducing the risks of nuclear accident (or incident). Three considerations have priority: the siting of nuclear power stations; the transport and storage of nuclear waste; and the desirability of reprocessing spent nuclear fuel.

Where possible, nuclear plants are located well away from large urban areas (Figure 7.4). However, this is difficult in small, densely populated countries such as the UK and Japan. Because of public opposition to the nuclear industry, new stations are often built on existing nuclear sites.

Management plans must deal with the problem of safe transport and storage of radioactive waste. In the UK, highly radioactive waste is stored on the surface at Sellafield in Cumbria. However, this is only a temporary solution. With the risk of accidental leakage and terrorist attack, a secure underground repository will eventually be needed. Yet, despite more than 50 years of operation, the British nuclear industry has still to find a suitable location for permanent and safe storage for its nuclear waste underground.

Governments also have to choose whether to store or reprocess **spent nuclear fuel**. **Reprocessing** recovers 97% of unspent uranium (as well as plutonium — the raw materials for nuclear weapons) which can then be recycled. But reprocessing is costly and produces the most toxic radioactive waste, adding to problems of storage.

Figure 7.4 Proposed and existing nuclear power sites in the UK

The advantages of nuclear power

Revised

Despite the environmental and health risks posed by nuclear power generation, in the past few years the case for the industry's expansion has strengthened. As a result, major investment in the nuclear option is expected in many western countries in the next decade. The arguments are that:

- countries such as the UK face an **energy gap**, as old nuclear power stations, built in the 1960s and 1970s, are decommissioned
- nuclear energy does not emit GHGs and sulphur dioxide and its expansion will help countries meet international obligations to combat global warming, climate change and acid rain. This makes nuclear power 'green' and therefore environmentally more sustainable
- nuclear technology has become more reliable and safer
- proven reserves of uranium are sufficient to last for just 60–70 years but estimated reserves should meet current rates of demand (4 million tonnes/year) for the next 250 years.

However, following the nuclear accident at Fukushima in northeast Honshu in 2011 (the first major accident since Chernobyl) western governments have reassessed the nuclear option, reviewing its hazards and political acceptability.

The use of fossil fuels

Acid rain   Revised

Acid rain is an unwanted side-effect of industrial development, and specifically the consumption of fossil fuels. Its effects are worldwide — hence its description as a **transboundary environmental problem**.

Causes of acid rain

Acid rain is caused by emissions of sulphur dioxide (SO_2), nitrogen oxides (NO_x) and ammonia. In the atmosphere these pollutants combine with water droplets to form sulphuric acid and nitric acid. Eventually the chemicals reach the ground in precipitation, or as **dry depositions**.

The main sources of pollutants responsible for acid rain are:

- coal-fired power stations and heavy processing industries such as iron and steel, which emit sulphur dioxide
- motor vehicles, which emit nitrogen oxide as exhaust gases
- intensive livestock farming and organic fertilisers, which emit ammonia

The impact of acid rain

The main effects of acid rain are environmental and include:

- acidification of lakes, streams and soils
- destruction of forests and wildlife (particularly aquatic life)
- corrosion of stone buildings and stone monuments (limestone, sandstone)

When soils become acidified they **leach** essential plant nutrients and release toxic metals, such as aluminium. These metals enter food chains and threaten wildlife. For example, dissolved aluminium and acid water kill aquatic invertebrates such as water snails, mayfly larvae and dragonflies, which support an array of birds, fish and aquatic mammals. Forests also suffer extensive damage. By the 1980s almost one-quarter of all trees in Europe showed some damage due to acid rain. The environmental impact of acid rain is most severe in uplands where rainfall is high and soils and rocks contain little free calcium to neutralise acidity.

Management

In the EU the acid rain problem has been tackled successfully by international treaties and agreements. They have led to drastic reductions in emissions of sulphur dioxide, nitrogen and ammonia. For example, a 43% cut in EU sulphur dioxide emissions was achieved between 1990 and 2002.

Worldwide, emissions that cause acid rain have risen since 2000. This is largely due to the growth of the Chinese economy, which relies on coal. For China, acid rain is part of the environmental cost of the country's soaring economic growth. However, China is taking steps to manage the problem. Policies for dealing with acid rain include charging polluters for sulphur dioxide emissions, installing desulphurisation equipment in power stations (coal-fired power stations produce two-thirds of China's sulphur dioxide emissions), and burning better quality (i.e. low sulphur) coal.

> **Typical mistake**
>
> Do not conflate the causes of acid rain and global warming. Acid rain results from emissions of sulphur dioxide, nitrogen dioxide and ammonia. Global warming is due to atmospheric pollution by GHGs (e.g. carbon dioxide).

The exhaustion of fossil fuels

Fossil fuels are finite resources that form on timescales measuring tens of millions of years. As rates of fossil fuel consumption easily outstrip rates of formation, at current rates of use coal, oil and gas could be exhausted within 50–200 years (Table 7.3).

Table 7.3 World fossil fuel reserves and reserve-to-production (R/P) ratios 2009

	Reserves	R/P ratios
Oil	1333.1 billion barrels	45.7 years
Natural gas	2.21 trillion m³	62.8 years
Coal	826 billion tonnes	242.4 years

Typical mistake

It is a common misconception to think that reserves of oil and gas will be exhausted in the near future. In the past 50 years rates of consumption have been matched by the discovery of new reserves and more efficient extraction of existing reserves. In 2009, reserves of both oil and gas increased.

Now test yourself

6 Make a list of the ways in which energy cartels, international political conflicts and TNCs influence oil supplies.

7 State three reasons why international movements of oil and gas are vulnerable to terrorist attack.

8 Construct a table with rows for renewable and non-renewable energy resources. For each type of energy list their adverse environmental effects.

9 Make a list in tabular form of the arguments for and against the expansion of nuclear power.

10 List, as a series of bullet points, the causes and consequences of acid rain pollution.

Answers on p. 125

Sustainable energy supplies

Sustainable energy

Sustainable energy is renewable, because it is either recyclable (e.g. hydro power) or inexhaustible (e.g. solar power). It is also either **carbon-free** (e.g. wind power) or **carbon neutral** (e.g. biofuels). Around 13% of the world's primary energy production is renewable, although most of this is wood used for cooking and heating in developing countries. Only 2.8% of global energy comes from **alternative energy** sources such as HEP, wind, solar, tidal and wave power. A major expansion of alternative energy is currently underway in many developed countries.

Carbon neutral means that electricity from biomass resources releases the same amount of carbon that trees and other plants absorb through photosynthesis during their growth.

Hydroelectric power

Hydroelectric power or HEP is the most popular type of alternative energy. In Europe it dominates the energy economies of Norway, Sweden, Switzerland and Austria. Many developing countries in Asia, Africa and South America also rely heavily on HEP. Massive projects include those at Three Gorges on the Yangzte River in China and at Itaipú on the Paraná River in South America. Ideal physical conditions for HEP generation are:

- powerful rivers with high annual discharges such as the Yangzte and the Congo (large catchments, high precipitation)

- steep gradients (e.g. overdeepened valleys in glaciated uplands)

- natural storage reservoirs such as lakes, glaciers and icefields

Typical mistake

Remember that renewable energy, although not always used sustainably, is more important in the developing than in the developed world.

HEP is renewable, carbon-free and has the potential to generate enormous amounts of electricity. However, there are issues concerning its sustainability. Most schemes involve the construction of dams. Upstream, vast areas are flooded, destroying habitats, wildlife, farmland and even settlements. Downstream, dams change the character and behaviour of rivers (e.g. colder clearer water, absence of floods), modifying habitats and damaging aquatic ecosystems. Additional problems include the huge capital outlay needed to build large dams and their questionable benefits to local people whose livelihoods and homes may be at risk (e.g. flooded valleys, loss of fisheries).

Wind power — Revised ☐

The amount of energy generated by wind power depends on wind speed, air density, the spacing of wind turbines and the size of turbine blades. The UK, committed to generating 15% of all its electricity from renewables by 2020, will rely mainly on the expansion of wind power to meet this target. However, there is considerable hostility to **wind farms** in the UK because:

- they take up large tracts of land (i.e. 7 ha for every megawatt of electricity produced)
- they are visually intrusive, often being sited prominently on hills and ridges where wind speeds are highest
- many of the best sites (e.g. coasts and uplands) have protected or high environmental status
- they cause high bird mortality through collisions with turbines and transmission lines

As a result, many planning applications for wind farms on mainland sites are rejected, and others may be delayed for years. Energy companies have responded by locating new wind farms offshore (e.g. in the Thames estuary, the Wash and Morecambe Bay). A new generation of wind turbines with blades up to 150 m in diameter is being sited offshore, where they are less intrusive and therefore less controversial.

> **Typical mistake**
>
> Renewable energy is not the same as environmentally friendly energy. Hydro, wind and tidal power can all have significant adverse environmental effects.

Solar power — Revised ☐

Electricity is generated by solar power in two ways:
- by boiling water to produce steam which drives turbines
- by using arrays of **photovoltaic (PV) cells**

Ideal conditions for solar power are found in desert regions in the tropics and subtropics, where skies are clear for at least 300 days a year and solar radiation is intense. Invariably, these areas are sparsely populated and so there are few objectors. Although the development of solar power is still in its infancy, its scope is huge. For example, an area the size of Portugal in the Sahara Desert could produce electricity equal to the combined output of all the world's power stations. To date, major investments have been limited to southern Spain and California's Mojave Desert.

Tidal energy — Revised ☐

Tidal power is a great untapped source of renewable energy. Ideal generating conditions are found in estuaries with large tidal ranges (e.g. 8–10 m) and where barrages can be built at relatively low cost. The UK has huge tidal energy potential

Exam practice answers and quick quizzes at **www.therevisionbutton.co.uk/myrevisionnotes**

at several locations, such the Severn estuary, Morecambe Bay and Strangford Lough.

Apart from the enormous capital costs, the main problem with tidal power is its environmental impact. Constructing a barrage across an estuary destroys salt-water tidal habitats (e.g. salt marshes, mudflats) and entire ecosystems. Feeding areas for migrant birds are lost, as well as spawning areas for fish, and habitats for marine invertebrates. In the UK, a further obstacle is the legally protected status of most large estuaries, which are **wetlands** of international importance. Barrages also have economic disbenefits, such as disrupting navigation and destroying inshore fisheries.

Wave energy

Revised

Wave energy is a sustainable, carbon-free source of energy. Unlike wind, which is intermittent, waves are generated in even the calmest conditions. The UK, with its long coastline and stormy coastal waters, is well-placed to exploit wave energy. Already a number of experimental plants operate in the Western and Northern Isles. However, the technology has still to be perfected and electricity generation on a commercial scale is still some years away.

Biomass fuels

Revised

Wood is the most important biomass fuel. Mainly used for cooking and heating in the developing world, it accounts for around 10% of global primary energy use. Providing annual consumption does not exceed annual rates of growth, wood is a sustainable fuel. Other biomass fuels widely used in LEDCs include animal dung and vegetable waste.

The UK's first wood-burning power plant is in operation near Lockerbie in Scotland. It burns 470,000 tonnes of sustainable wood fuel a year, including 95,000 tonnes of fast-growing willow saplings harvested on a three-year rotation. The plant will save 140,000 tonnes of GHG emissions a year. Similar biomass power stations are currently under construction at Sheffield and Portbury, near Bristol.

Appropriate technology for sustainable development

Revised

In many LEDCs small-scale development projects based on **appropriate technology** are the most effective means to improve levels of human wellbeing. The main feature of appropriate technologies is their simplicity. They rely on local energy resources such as biofuels, draught animals and human labour, as well as traditional skills and know-how. In contrast, technologically advanced schemes, such as major dam construction, often do little to improve the lives of local people.

In northern China, centuries of overgrazing and overcutting of trees caused widespread deforestation, soil erosion and loss of biodiversity. Reafforestation in the Korqin Sandy Lands region of northern China aims to halt land degradation and provide local inhabitants with a sustainable source of fuelwood and timber. Millions of fast-growing poplar and pine trees have been planted as shelter belts to protect farmland, stabilise soils and give local people a sustainable source of timber for fuel and building. The newly planted trees also provide fodder for livestock, which allows sustainable grazing of the rangelands.

Energy conservation

The first step to achieving a sustainable energy economy is to reduce energy consumption and carbon emissions. Governments play a major role in promoting **energy conservation** and moving towards a low carbon economy.

Now test yourself

11 What is the difference between (a) renewable and sustainable energy, (b) carbon-free and carbon neutral energy?

12 Why can fossil fuels never be used sustainably?

13 What are the environmental advantages of renewable forms of energy?

14 What are the environmental disadvantages of renewables?

Answers on p. 126

Homes and workplaces
Revised

Domestic demand accounts for nearly one-third of primary energy consumption in the UK, and service activities (offices) nearly 16%. Energy conservation in homes and workplaces aims to reduce energy consumption, mainly through energy conservation, and at the same time reduce carbon emissions. In the UK new houses and workplaces must conform to building regulations that include, for example, minimum standards of heat insulation and limits on the ratio of window/doorspace area to floor area. Energy performance certificates are required for all new buildings completed since 2008. The UK government also provides grants for loft insulation, and pays householders who generate their own electricity from renewables such as solar and wind power. Figure 7.5 shows a home designed to reduce energy loss, and generate energy from solar panels and a heat exchanger. Other factors that influence energy conservation are aspect (i.e. Sun-facing), the size and placement of windows to maximise solar gain, and the installation of smart energy meters.

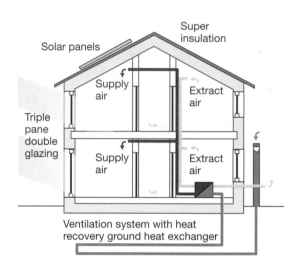

Figure 7.5 House designed for maximum energy efficiency

Transport for sustainability
Revised

Domestic transport is responsible for over one-quarter of UK energy consumption and one-fifth of GHG emissions. If we include international air transport and shipping, the proportion is even higher. The government plans to cut emissions from transport by 14% on 2008 levels by 2020.

Among the government initiatives designed to create more **sustainable transport** in the UK by 2020 are:

● more fuel-efficient vehicles — smaller cars with more efficient engines pay lower road tax

● electric vehicles — in 2010 the government introduced a £5,000 subsidy for new electric cars

● resources for cycling — more cycle lanes and cycle stores at transport hubs (e.g. train stations)

● more funding for rail and bus transport — to increase capacity (before the 2011 cuts government planned to invest £10 billion in the railways)

Case study Managing energy supply in the UK

Aims UK energy policy aims to achieve: (a) security of supply, (b) reduced carbon emissions, and (c) improved energy conservation and efficiency.

Security of energy supply The UK is no longer self-sufficient in energy. To meet this energy gap (i.e. demand exceeding supply) and secure energy supplies, the government plans to: (1) rely on a diverse range of energy types — fossil fuels, nuclear, alternative energy, (2) develop new resources and new types of energy. The UK will continue to rely on imported coal, oil and gas, while exploring new offshore oil and gas deposits west of Shetland. Ten new nuclear power stations will be built and should be operational by the early 2020s. Most will be sited on existing nuclear sites. Government targets are for the UK to produce 15% of the country's energy from sustainable sources (mainly wind power) by 2020.

Reducing carbon emissions Energy production is a major contributor to GHG emissions. The Climate Change Act of 2008 committed the UK to reduce its GHG emissions by 34% in 2020 and 80% by 2050. By 2020, 40% of the UK's electricity should come from low carbon sources — renewables, nuclear and fossil fuels from power plants fitted with carbon capture/storage technologies.

Energy conservation A range of measures have been introduced to make new and existing homes, offices and transport more energy efficient. Financial incentives are available to households investing in renewable energy such as solar panels and small wind turbines.

Case study Managing energy supply in China

Aims China's energy policies, delivered in the government's five-year plans, aim to achieve: (a) accelerated domestic energy production to meet rising demand and avoid power shortages, (b) conservation of energy — more efficient and less intensive use, and (c) development of renewable energy resources.

Increase domestic energy production China achieved massive increases in all types of domestic energy production between 1999 and 2009 to feed the growing demand of its booming economy. Coal output increased two and a half times, gas threefold, and nuclear by nearly five times. Meanwhile, CO_2 emissions more than doubled. Spectacular increases were also achieved in renewables: China is the world's leading producer of HEP with over 200 GW of capacity (recent completion of the Three Gorges Dam and Yellow River projects). This will double by 2020. A huge expansion of wind power (though from a low base) has also

occurred since 1999, making China the world's second biggest producer of wind power.

Energy conservation China plans to move away from energy-intensive industries and its smokestack economy towards a more service-based economy. It also plans to rely more on cleaner energy supplies, with a tenfold increase in nuclear capacity by 2020. By 2020, 15% of China's energy demand should be met from HEP and wind power.

Environment China's priority remains economic growth, though as prosperity increases more attention is given to the environment. China is currently the world's largest emitter of CO_2 and other GHGs. Industry consumes 70% of electricity production; domestic consumption is just 10%. More efficient and less polluting coal-fired power stations with coal gasification and carbon capture are planned, and the renewables sector will grow much more rapidly than fossil fuels.

Check your understanding

1   Outline the factors that influence a country's energy mix.
2   How does the global production of and trade in crude oil affect geopolitics?
3   Compare the advantages of coal and nuclear power as energy sources.
4   Argue the case for the expansion of nuclear energy in the UK.
5   What is meant by the 'energy gap' and why is it an important issue in the UK?

Answers on p. 126

Exam practice

1 (a) Study Figure 7.3 which shows world coal production. Describe the pattern shown in Figure 7.3. [4]

(b) Outline the environmental impact of coal as a source of energy. [5]

(c) Study Figure 7.4 which shows the location of existing and proposed nuclear power station sites in the UK. Describe and explain the factors that influence the location of nuclear power stations. [6]

(d) Examine the arguments for and against the expansion of nuclear power to meet future energy demands. [15]

2 (a) Study Figures 7.1 and 7.2, which show the energy mix of Sweden and India, respectively. Outline the factors that are likely to influence a country's energy mix. [5]

(b) Describe recent changes in global patterns of energy supply and consumption. [4]

(c) Explain how geopolitics influences the production of, and international trade in, oil. [6]

(d) Discuss the view that renewable energy has more positive than negative implications for the environment. [15]

Answers and quick quiz 7 online

Online

Examiner's summary

✔ Energy types can be split into renewables and non-renewables, and primary and secondary energy.

✔ When explaining a country's energy mix, it is important to cover a range of economic, political and environmental factors.

✔ It is important to support general discussion with reference to specific and detailed examples.

✔ Remember that most estimates of fossil fuel reserves are only approximate and are likely to change in future as new resources are discovered and new technologies developed.

✔ All forms of energy production and use have adverse environmental effects, which vary in scale and severity.

✔ A balanced approach is needed to evaluate the arguments for and against nuclear energy.

✔ The distinction between the causes of acid rain and global warming should be understood.

✔ The continued dependence of rural populations in the developing world on renewable (biomass) energy should be appreciated.

✔ Fossil fuels are likely to dominate the global energy economy for at least the next 30 years.

✔ Remember that renewable energy is not always the same as sustainable energy.

8 Health issues

Global health patterns

Life expectancy at birth, **mortality** and **morbidity** are key indicators of the overall health status of a population.

> **Mortality** is the incidence of death in a population.
>
> **Morbidity** is ill-health that reduces efficiency and the ability to work.

Mortality Revised

Life expectancy at birth, influenced by a range of economic, social and environmental factors (e.g. diet, water supply, sanitation and healthcare), is an effective summary of living standards in a society. The biggest single determinant of life expectancy is childhood mortality. Children (along with the elderly) are particularly susceptible to illness, with one-fifth of all deaths globally occurring in children under 5 years.

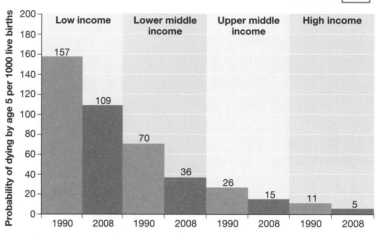

Figure 8.1 Childhood mortality under 5 years and economic status

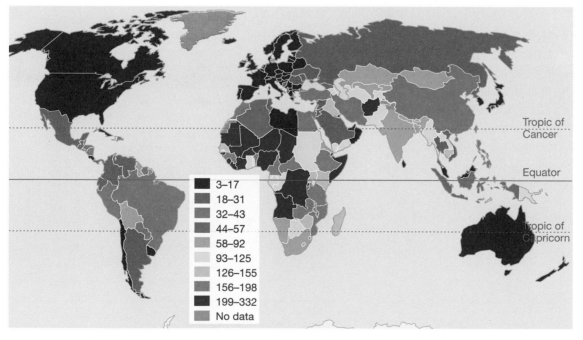

Figure 8.2 Distribution of childhood mortality under 5 years (per 1000 live births)

Figures 8.1 and 8.2, compiled by the World Health Organisation (WHO), show under-5 mortality rates for low, lower-middle, upper-middle and high-income countries. The main global patterns of child mortality by income are:

- high-income countries have lower levels of child mortality than poorer ones, e.g. 5/1,000 deaths in high-income countries by the age of 5, compared with 157/1,000 in low-income countries

- a few low- and middle-income countries have achieved levels of child mortality comparable to rich countries (e.g. Cuba 6/1,000)

Child mortality rates have fallen in all types of country since 1990, though rates of decline have been least in low-income countries. The concentration of low-income countries in Africa (especially sub-Saharan Africa) results in this region having child mortality rates double those of other less developed regions (Table 8.1). Meanwhile, rates of child mortality in the developed world — Europe, the Americas, western Pacific — are barely one-eighth of those in Africa.

Table 8.1 Rates of child mortality (under 5s) per 1000 in 2008 (source WHO)

Region	Under-5 mortality rate/1,000
Africa	142
Americas	18
Southeast Asia	63
Europe	14
Eastern Mediterranean	78
West Pacific	21

Typical mistake

Death rates (number of deaths/1,000 population/year) are not strictly speaking mortality. Because age structure has a strong influence on the death rate, death rates give a misleading impression of health/ill-health in a population.

Average life expectancy values should be viewed critically. In poor societies with high infant mortality, life expectancies are often misleadingly low.

Morbidity

Revised

Morbidity concerns ill-health, and is often related to chronic diseases such as malaria, tuberculosis (TB) and HIV/AIDS. Although mortality rates associated with such diseases are high, diseases such as malaria and TB result in debilitating long-term illness which seriously hinders economic progress.

Malaria and TB are responsible for high levels of morbidity throughout the developing world. For example, the prevalence of TB is 50 times greater in low-income than in high-income countries. HIV is highest in Africa, where rates of prevalence among adults aged 15–49 years are ten times higher than European and American levels. The highest rates of HIV/AIDS are in southern Africa, with around one-quarter of the adult population in South Africa, Botswana and Lesotho infected. High morbidity rates are often related to poverty (e.g. overcrowding, poor diets), inadequate healthcare and poor education.

Overall levels of morbidity can be summarised by **healthy life expectancy** (HLE) at birth. HLE measures the number of years on average that a person can expect to live in good health. Some examples are given in Table 8.2.

Table 8.2 Healthy life expectancy at birth (years) in 2008 (source WHO)

Country	HLE (years — both sexes)
Norway	74
UK	72
USA	70
Sri Lanka	65
Ethiopia	50
Afghanistan	36
Sierra Leone	34

Case study   HIV/AIDS — an infectious disease

Epidemiology The Human Immunodeficiency Virus (HIV) is transmitted by the exchange of body fluids (e.g. blood, semen) most often through sexual contact. The virus damages the immune system, making the body susceptible to illness and infection. Disease caused by HIV damage to the immune system is known as Acquired Immune Deficiency Syndrome or AIDS.

Worldwide, 33 million people were infected with HIV in 2009 (Figure 8.3). In the same year, AIDS-related illnesses caused 1.8 million deaths. Since 1981, an estimated 25 million people have died from AIDS, most of them in sub-Saharan Africa.

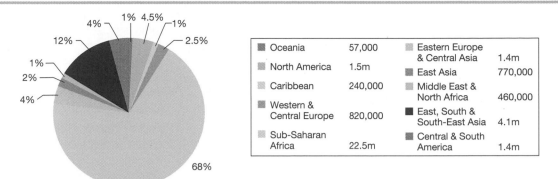

Figure 8.3 HIV infection by region

■ Oceania	57,000	■	Eastern Europe & Central Asia	1.4m
■ North America	1.5m	■	East Asia	770,000
■ Caribbean	240,000	■	Middle East & North Africa	460,000
■ Western & Central Europe	820,000	■	East, South & South-East Asia	4.1m
■ Sub-Saharan Africa	22.5m	■	Central & South America	1.4m

Demographic impact Because of HIV/AIDS, life expectancy will continue to fall throughout southern Africa: in Botswana from 67 to 54 years 1990–2015; in South Africa from 65 years to 50 years during the same period. Meanwhile, high mortality among young adults has caused a decline in birth rates and an overall slowdown, and in some cases an absolute decrease, of population (e.g. Botswana, South Africa, Namibia). Without the HIV/AIDS epidemic, South Africa's population in 2015 would have reached 54 million — 10 million more than is forecast. Changes in mortality and fertility have also impacted age structure, with large percentage shrinkages by 2015 in the 0–15 and 30–65 age groups.

Economic impact The prevalence of HIV/AIDS has damaged the economies of several African countries and in some has reversed economic development. Most HIV/AIDS sufferers are adults between 15 and 49 years, i.e. the most economically active and productive part of the workforce. On an individual household level, HIV/AIDS results in loss of income, indebtedness, and increases the likelihood of poverty. In sub-Saharan Africa, the HIV/AIDS epidemic has reduced GDP by an average 1.5% per year and in east Africa absenteeism due to illness may have cut business profits by 6–8%. Premature deaths have reduced the labour supply and raised labour costs; while increased morbidity has lowered productivity and profits. In rural areas HIV/AIDS has led to the neglect and abandonment of agricultural work, diminishing food output and increasing food insecurity.

Social impact Premature mortality from AIDS has destroyed millions of families. Orphaned children often have to assume family responsibilities in households with few if any savings or assets. Others have to leave school to care for dying parents. In countries worst affected by AIDS, taking care of the sick imposes huge financial burdens and overwhelms already inadequate national health services. In southern Africa more than half of all hospital beds are occupied by AIDS sufferers.

Case study Diabetes — 'a disease of affluence'

Epidemiology Diabetes is caused by a deficiency of insulin, a hormone secreted by the pancreas. Insulin enables glucose to enter cells and provide energy. It also keeps blood sugar levels within safe limits. Globally, the disease afflicts nearly 250 million people.

Type 2 diabetes, although found worldwide, is often seen as a 'disease of affluence' associated with lifestyles in the developed world. Globally, diabetes is responsible for 3.8 million deaths a year — more than twice the number who die from AIDS. In MEDCs the recent rapid increase in the number of cases has been called a diabetes epidemic. The disease is more concentrated in poorer communities and is closely linked to obesity, which in turn is related to the consumption of low-cost, high calorie, convenience foods and drinks and lack of physical exercise.

Distribution Diabetes is widespread in the developed and less developed world, but is most strongly concentrated in North America, Europe and the Middle East. Originally diabetes was a disease of the elderly, but in recent decades it has become increasingly common in younger adults of working age and even children.

The spread of the disease By 2026, it is estimated that the disease will affect 380 million people. This is consistent with rising levels of obesity throughout the developed and developing world. Currently in the USA, 12.3% of the population aged 20–79 years are diabetic (12.3%). Other countries with similar high rates include Saudi Arabia (13.6%) and Germany (12%). In contrast, some of the poorest countries in the world, such as Ethiopia and Kenya, have low rates (2.8% and 2.0%, respectively).

Economic impact The economic impact of diabetes (which leads to medical complications, such as heart disease, stroke, blindness and kidney failure) includes the costs of healthcare and prevention, loss of life, disability, reduced earnings, and lost economic growth. Currently these costs are spiralling. In 2007 the cost of the disease worldwide was US$290 billion. This is expected to increase to US$380 billion by 2025. More than 80% of spending on medical care for diabetes is in MEDCs. Investment in diabetes care and prevention is lowest in the poorest countries. With economic development and rising obesity, a huge increase in the disease is likely in future in countries such as China and India.

Food and health

To remain healthy, people need a sufficient calorie intake and a balanced diet. In 2010 the UN estimated that 950 million people did not have enough to eat and that 60% of all child deaths were due to poor nutrition — 98% of them in the developing world.

Undernutrition and malnutrition

Revised

In some parts of the developing world, and especially in sub-Saharan Africa, chronic food shortages result in **undernutrition** and **malnutrition**. Poverty is the root cause of undernutrition and malnutrition. Undernutrition is the condition where dietary energy intake is below the minimum required to maintain a healthy life and is most widespread among the poorest groups in LEDCs. Severe undernutrition eventually leads to death by starvation. However, far more common is chronic undernourishment, which weakens the immune system and puts individuals at risk from infectious illnesses such as diarrhoea and pneumonia. The World Health Organisation (WHO) estimates that worldwide one-quarter of all children below 5 years of age are underweight and that half of all childhood deaths in LEDCs are due to undernutrition.

Malnutrition is caused by an unbalanced diet, most often resulting in a deficiency of protein, fat and essential vitamins. Like undernutrition, it has a direct influence on ill-health. Poverty means that people are unable to afford more expensive foods such as meat, vegetables and fruit essential to a balanced diet. Diets high in carbohydrates (e.g. starchy crops such as cassava and yams) but low in protein are responsible for **kwashiorkor**, a disease which is often fatal in children, and **beriberi**, caused by a dietary absence of vitamin B$_1$. Malnutrition, and the absence of essential vitamins, iron deficiency and iodine deficiency, **stunt** the physical growth of nearly 200 million children in the developing world.

Obesity

Revised

Overnutrition causes **obesity** and excessive accumulations of body fat. Obesity is associated with major health risks such as diabetes, heart disease and cancer. Excessive weight is measured by the **body mass index** (BMI). This is calculated by dividing a person's weight in kilograms by the square of their height in metres. A BMI of 25–29.9 suggests a person is overweight; 30 and above defines obesity. Using this measure, the WHO estimates that 1.5 billion people worldwide are overweight, and 500 million are obese. Although obesity is most prevalent in rich countries, a dramatic rise in obesity is currently taking place in many low- and middle-income countries. The main reasons for this trend are:

- increased consumption of energy-dense foods, high in fat and sugar
- decreased physical activity

Famine Revised

Famine is a widespread food shortage that leads to a sharp rise in mortality. However, the concept of famine is not as simple as it might appear. For example, famines are often highly localised and may affect only one social or economic group. Famines are also not always the result of an absolute shortage of food. They can occur when a breakdown in the marketing system occurs or when people simply cannot afford to buy the food that is available. In famines, starvation is rarely the cause of death. Most often, undernutrition reduces the body's resistance to disease and people die from a range of infections.

Famines can have several causes:

- severe reduction in food production due to harvest failure (e.g. drought in the Horn of Africa in the mid-1990s)
- political instability that disrupts food production (e.g. China's Great Leap Forward in the early 1960s)
- overexploitation of declining soil and water resources as a result of rising population levels (e.g. Niger in 2005)
- natural disasters in developing countries, such as tropical cyclones that destroy crops (e.g. Cyclone Nargis in Myanmar in 2008)

> **Typical mistake**
> It is simplistic to think that famines result from an absolute shortage of food in a country or society. Famines most often affect specific groups of people (e.g. the poor) who have the least purchasing power and therefore the greatest food insecurity.

Healthcare approaches

The influence of stage of economic development Revised

Countries at different stages of economic development often have contrasting approaches to delivering healthcare services. Such contrasts are evident in the examples of Cuba, a lower-middle income country, and Haiti, one of the poorest countries in the world.

Case study — Healthcare in Cuba

Background Cuba is a lower-middle income country. In 2010 its GDP per capita was just below US$10,000, similar to Tunisia and Peru, giving it a world ranking of 109th. Its population was 11 million in 2011, and is expected to remain stable for the next 15–20 years.

Healthcare system Cuba's modern healthcare system was established in the 1970s — the outcome of a socialist political system where government-funded healthcare is a right guaranteed to all citizens. Along with food, clothing, housing and education, the delivery of healthcare has the highest priority.

Primary healthcare is the foundation of the system, which employs 33,000 doctors. There are 498 polyclinics that each serve between 30,000 and 60,000 people. They are similar to outpatient departments in small hospitals and provide specialist consultation and diagnostic procedures (e.g. screening, ultrasound, endoscopy). At the grassroots level, basic medical services are provided by neighbourhood-based family doctor and nurses' offices. They serve around 2,500 patients each and deliver the bulk of health services. Secondary healthcare comprises large municipal and regional hospitals. The emphasis of the Cuban healthcare system is on preventative medicine through primary care.

Achievements Despite limited resources, Cuba's healthcare system in the past 40 years has been an outstanding success. Average life expectancy (77 years) is comparable with many high-income countries. Child mortality rates for under 5s (6/1,000), and maternal mortality rates (7/100,000) even exceed those in Canada and Australia. TB rates are just 2/100,000 and malaria has been eradicated.

Background Although less than 100 km separate the island state of Haiti from Cuba, the economic and demographic disparities between them are huge. Haiti is a low-income country, the poorest in the western hemisphere — more like sub-Saharan Africa than the Caribbean. GDP per capita in 2010 was US$717 and on the UN's human development index it ranked 145th out of 169 countries. 80% of the population live in poverty. Haiti's population is forecast to increase from 9.7 million in 2011 to nearly 12 million by 2030.

Healthcare system Haiti has been an independent state since 1804, yet its healthcare system is rudimentary. This is not only due to poverty, but also to long-term political instability and natural hazards (earthquakes, hurricanes). The few health services that exist have declined over the past two decades. There are serious shortages of trained medical staff (only 1,000 doctors in the whole country), medical supplies and poor management of clinics and hospitals. Spending on healthcare in 2008 was only US$85 per person. Increasingly, healthcare relies on charities and a patchwork of foreign agencies such as Médecins Sans Frontières, which offer free clinics. The healthcare infrastructure of clinics and hospitals is totally inadequate to meet the needs of the population. In the capital, Port au Prince, government healthcare services are practically non-existent, while private healthcare is beyond the means of all but a tiny minority. Many are forced to rely on traditional healing.

Outcome Poverty, political conflict and poor governance have created an appalling healthcare situation in Haiti. Malnutrition is widespread and nearly 140,000 children die from preventable diseases (TB, malaria, pneumonia) every year. Average life expectancy is 62 years; rates of mortality among children under 5 years is 12 times greater than in neighbouring Cuba, while maternal mortality is nearly 100 times higher. TB rates are 290/100,000 and malaria causes nearly 37,000 deaths a year.

Typical mistake

Avoid generalisation and stereotypes in examination answers. The Cuban example shows that effective healthcare systems are not just confined to high-income countries.

Transnational corporations and health

Transnational corporations (TNCs) are large companies that produce or source goods and services internationally and market them worldwide. Their role in developing, manufacturing and marketing pharmaceutical products and consumables such as tobacco, fast food and soft drinks has a significant impact on human health.

TNCs and the sale of life-saving drugs

Revised

Diseases such as malaria, TB and HIV/AIDS cause massive suffering and premature death throughout the developing world. Malaria, endemic in 109 countries, killed 863,000 people in 2009. Yet, life expectancy and morbidity could be improved for millions of people if they had access to affordable drugs. Pharmaceutical TNCs based in MEDCs, however, control the manufacture and sales of these drugs. Their priority is profit and recouping their expenditure on research and development. As a result, many life-saving drugs, patented by pharmaceutical TNCs, cannot be manufactured cheaply under licence in LEDCs and are unaffordable to millions of people in the developing world. Furthermore, because profit margins for selling drugs in poorer countries are small, there is limited incentive for pharmaceutical TNCs to develop new drugs for this market.

TNCs and the globalisation of food systems

Revised

Tobacco

Many TNCs manufacture and market food and other consumables knowing they are injurious to human health. The most obvious example is tobacco. Worldwide, approximately 1.3 billion people smoke cigarettes or other tobacco products. As the health risks from smoking in MEDCs are well known, the market for tobacco products in these countries has dwindled. Tobacco companies have responded by switching their attention to LEDCs. Today over 80% of smokers are in LEDCs and the numbers are increasing rapidly. If unchecked, this will create huge health problems in the future. By 2030, around 10 million people a year could die from smoking-related illness; and 70% of these deaths will be in LEDCs.

Unhealthy food and drink

With sales stagnant in North America and Europe, in 2006 Coca Cola turned to emerging markets in the developing world to boost its profits and growth. Similarly, fast food chains have successfully promoted foods high in sugar and saturated fats in LEDCs. Supported by intensive advertising, fast food is now a globalised industry, and expanding rapidly into markets in the developing world. The adverse effects on human health include obesity and increased risks of diet-related diseases.

Powdered milk

TNCs such as Nestlé have promoted the sale of powdered milk products for infants as a replacement for breast feeding. This has been hugely controversial. Breast feeding has physical benefits both for babies and mothers. It protects babies from obesity, asthma and chest infections, and mothers from various cancers and osteoporosis later in life. In the Philippines, food companies spend US$100 million a year advertising breast milk substitutes. The result is that only 16% of children aged between four and five months old are exclusively breastfed — a figure that has fallen by one-third since 1998. Reliance on powdered milk increases the risk of malnutrition in infants and increases pressure on the budgets of families who are already poor. According to the WHO, every year 16,000 Filipino children die as a result of feeding with substitutes for breast milk.

> **Examiner's tip**
>
> The activities of TNCs in promoting global health are controversial. As always, a balanced appreciation of their role is needed. Any adverse effects on human health (see above) must be offset against their positive influence through investment, employment and economic growth.

Health and morbidity in the UK

Regional variations   Revised

Geographical inequalities in health and morbidity rates are found in the UK at a regional scale. The main features of these inequalities are:

- a north–south divide
- poorer than average rates in Scotland, Northern Ireland and northern England (and Wales)
- above-average rates in southern and eastern England
- average rates in the English Midlands

However, some aspects of health are not consistent with the north–south divide. For instance, levels of childhood obesity are above average in London, drug use is high in the southeast region, and the incidence of breast cancer is high in the southwest.

A clear north–south divide is evident for **standardised mortality rates** in the UK (Figure 8.4). Figure 8.4 shows detailed health patterns at subregional scale. The main features of this subregional geography are:

- high mortality levels in large urban centres such as Greater Manchester, Merseyside, Tyneside, South Yorkshire, central Scotland and south Wales (e.g. in

> **Standardised mortality rates** are measures adjusted for the age structure of population. They provide a more accurate measure of mortality and health than death rates.

southeast and southwest England, men have a 71% chance of living to 75 years; in Manchester, the chances are just 53%)

● higher mortality rates in urban areas, compared with rural areas

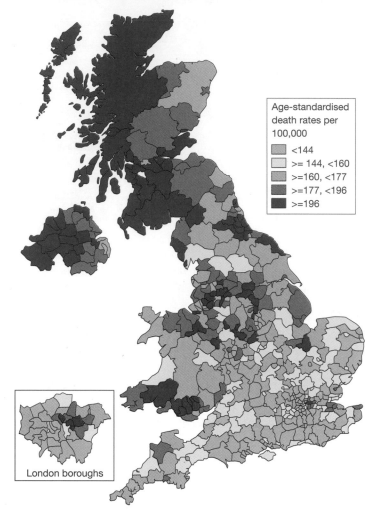

Figure 8.4 Standardised mortality rates in the UK

Intra-urban variations — Revised

Sharp geographical contrasts in health and morbidity also exist *within* cities in the UK. In inner London the highest rates of infant mortality are concentrated in Southwark, Newham, Haringey and Brent. The rates in Southwark and Newham (7 per 1,000), two of inner London's poorest boroughs, are more than double those in affluent Richmond (3.1 per 1,000).

Factors affecting regional variations in health and morbidity

Income and poverty — Revised

In British cities the geographical distribution of ill-health is associated with low incomes and poverty, which have a direct effect on access to housing. Households with low incomes are constrained to occupy low-quality housing, mainly located in inner city areas and on peripheral local authority estates. These households often suffer **multiple deprivation**, including low pay, long-term unemployment, poor levels of education, high rates of crime and so on. Poverty is also responsible for a range of factors that increase health risks. They include unhealthy diets (causing obesity), stress (leading to excessive consumption of alcohol and tobacco) and lifestyle. Average life expectancy at birth in 2008 for men in Calton, an area of acute deprivation in Glasgow, was just 54 years. A few miles away, in the affluent suburb of Lenzie, life expectancy for men was 82 years. Similar factors, associated with poverty and lifestyles, also explain inequalities in health and morbidity at the regional scale in the UK.

Age structure

Revised

Age is the major determinant of health and morbidity. With the exception of young children, ill-health and morbidity increase with age. People in old age are most likely to suffer chronic, degenerative diseases such as cancer and cardio-vascular failure, and to live alone (3 million pensioners live alone in England). Also, with weaker immune systems, old people and children are more susceptible to respiratory illnesses such as common colds, influenza and bronchitis.

Environment and pollution

Revised

Environmental pollution is known to increase health risks. In the UK, leukaemia clusters have been linked to nuclear installations, although causality is hard to prove. On Teesside in northeast England, elevated rates of lung cancer in populations living close to steel, chemical and oil refining installations were found in the 1990s. Air pollution from these industrial sources was thought to be the most likely explanation.

Air pollution is a direct risk to human health. Incinerators are known to emit carcinogenic chemicals such as dioxins and PCBs. Acid rain can cause premature death from heart disease and lung disorders such as asthma and bronchitis. In the developing world, water supplies contaminated by sewage transmit cholera, typhoid and diarrhoeal diseases. Polluted drinking water is probably the main cause of ill-health and premature mortality in the sprawling slums of cities in Africa, Asia and Latin America.

> **Examiner's tip**
>
> Remember that elevated levels of mortality and morbidity between or within regions are most often due to a combination of factors (e.g. income, age, education) rather than a single cause. For example, an individual suffering health deprivation is also likely to suffer income, housing, employment, education etc., deprivation.

Education

Revised

Geographical contrasts in health and morbidity within countries are often connected to education. In LEDCs, millions of people are unaware of basic hygiene or the health risks caused by polluted drinking water. Ignorance of the epidemiology of malaria often allows stagnant water, the breeding ground for malarial mosquitoes, to exist alongside human settlements. In southern Africa, the HIV/AIDS risk is increased because so many people refuse to accept that the disease is transmitted by casual sexual behaviour.

In rich countries it is much harder to isolate the effects of education from poverty. However, people who are poorly educated on average are more likely to have unhealthy diets and less likely to appreciate the health benefits of regular physical activity. Drug abuse and obesity, both of which increase health risks, are also more prevalent among less educated groups.

Now test yourself

4 What is malnutrition?

5 What is undernutrition?

6 Give two causes of obesity.

7 How does the impact of famine vary across a society?

8 State three ways in which TNCs can adversely affect human health.

9 What are the main geographical differences in human health in the UK?

10 What factors account for geographical differences in human health in the UK?

Answers on p. 127

Access to healthcare, good nutrition and exercise

Income, age and gender are three factors that influence access to facilities for healthcare, good nutrition and exercise in the UK and other MEDCs.

Access to healthcare services
Revised

Elderly people are more likely to suffer deteriorating health and make greater demands on healthcare services. At the same time, accessing healthcare services is difficult for the elderly who often live alone and are less likely to drive or own a car. These problems cause particular hardship for elderly populations in rural areas, where GP surgeries and hospitals are widely dispersed. As a result, cancer patients in remote rural areas in Scotland are less likely to be diagnosed and have poorer survival rates than their urban counterparts. And as the UK's rural population ages, this problem is likely to get worse. Similar problems of access are found among low-income groups in rural Britain who cannot afford a car and where public transport is poor.

Examiner's tip

Note that inequality of access to healthcare services because of age contributes to health exclusion and multiple deprivation.

Good nutrition
Revised

Good nutrition, with a balanced diet that includes fresh fruit and vegetables, is essential to maintain good health. It is estimated that 3 million people in the UK suffer from malnutrition, and that it costs £13 billion a year to treat. Diet is strongly influenced by income. UK households with low incomes have to rely on cheaper foods (e.g. tinned, processed) rather than fresh foods. Elderly people, often poor and living in isolation, are most at risk.

Poor nutrition is often exacerbated in low-income neighbourhoods in towns and cities by an absence of retail outlets selling fresh food. Discount supermarkets (e.g. Aldi, Netto), budget stores and fast food shops in these areas often provide low-cost food, but with restricted choice, reflecting the limited purchasing power of local consumers.

Exercise

Revised

Regular, vigorous exercise makes a vital contribution to physical and mental wellbeing. At present only 37% of men and 24% of women in the UK are sufficiently active to gain any health benefit. Opportunities for either formal or informal exercise vary with income, place of residence and gender. Membership of health clubs and gyms is costly and may be beyond the means of low-income households. Access to public facilities such as swimming pools and parks may depend on place of residence. Place of residence also affects the potential for informal exercise. Middle–higher income groups, in the outer suburbs or close to open countryside, have greater opportunities for outdoor activities such as rambling and cycling. They are also more likely to access exercise through local golf clubs, tennis clubs, cricket clubs and so on. People — particularly women — living in inner city neighbourhoods, with more traffic and higher rates of crime, may feel unsafe exercising outdoors, especially after dark.

Case study The provision of local healthcare in South Lakeland

Background South Lakeland district covers the southern part of the Lake District, and Morecambe Bay in Cumbria. It has a population of only 105,000, much of it scattered at low density in small rural communities. Kendal is the largest town; the only other sizeable urban centres are Windermere and Ulverston. The region is relatively prosperous, with household incomes close to the national average and few areas of deprivation. Quality of life is high, with a large part of the area located in the Lake District national park. Standardised mortality rates are relatively low, with life expectancies of 79 years for males and 83 years for females.

Healthcare provision Primary healthcare is provided by 21 GP practices. Secondary care is available at Westmorland General Hospital in Kendal. For more specialist hospital treatment residents must travel to Lancaster.

Age structure 23% of the population in South Lakeland are aged 65 and over. This is well above the national average (16%) and is the highest in Cumbria. Ageing will continue in future. The aged structure is the result of out-migration by young people, and large influxes of retirees in the past 30 years.

Health issues Health issues centre on the large and growing proportion of elderly residents. Rates of degenerative illnesses such as cardio-vascular diseases and dementia are high by national standards. Access to healthcare for elderly patients living in isolated rural locations, and without access to private transport, is a problem. Many villages are more than 8 km from a GP surgery. Other health issues are common to other parts of the UK: excessive alcohol consumption, childhood obesity, low uptake levels for flu and MMR vaccines and responses to screening programmes (e.g. for types of cancer).

Health implications Ageing of the population will continue. By 2031, over one-third of the population will be 65 years and over. Large numbers of elderly people will live alone (as spouses die) increasing loneliness and the risk of depression. As the population is relatively affluent and life expectancy is well above the UK average, increasing numbers of old people are likely to suffer from mental illness and dementia in future. Already rates of dementia are higher than the national average, and a 60% increase is forecast by 2025. This has resource implications for social/care services as well as healthcare, and could place considerable burdens on the local NHS trust.

Now test yourself

11 How can the spatial distribution of population in an area affect access to healthcare services?

12 How does age and income affect access to healthcare services?

13 How can the geography of an area affect residents' fitness levels and exercise?

14 How are levels of nutrition affected by geography and household incomes?

15 Describe the age structure of South Lakeland and the health issues to which it gives rise.

Answers on p. 127

Check your understanding

1 Describe and explain the global distribution of (a) HIV/AIDS, (b) diabetes.
2 With reference to specific countries, describe contrasting approaches to healthcare.
3 Assess the relative importance of factors responsible for regional inequalities in health in the UK.

Answers on p. 127

Exam practice

1 Study Figure 8.1 which shows mortality for children under 5 years in 1990 and 2008 in countries grouped by income status, and Figure 8.2 which shows the global distribution of under 5 year old child mortality in 2008.

   (a) (i) Describe the pattern shown in Figure 8.2.   **[4]**

      (ii) Analyse the relationship between Figure 8.1 and Figure 8.2.   **[5]**

   (b) Describe the influence of one infectious disease on health and economic development.   **[6]**

   (c) Discuss the impact of TNCs on mortality and morbidity in a globalising world.

2 Study Figure 8.3 which shows HIV/AIDS infection by region in 2008.

   (a) (i) Describe the pattern shown in Figure 8.3.   **[4]**

      (ii) Outline the reasons for global variations in the geographical distribution of HIV/AIDS.   **[5]**

   (b) Assess the social and economic impact of HIV/AIDS in the economically developing world.   **[6]**

   (c) Discuss the effectiveness of approaches to healthcare in countries at different stages of development.   **[15]**

Answers and quick quiz 8 online

Online

Examiner's summary

✔ Long-term debilitating diseases such as malaria and HIV/AIDS, which produce high rates of morbidity, can have devastating economic consequences for individual households and society.

✔ Death rates are not the same as mortality and are heavily influenced by age structure.

✔ Average life expectancy can be a misleading measure of mortality in societies that suffer high rates of infant mortality.

✔ Examination questions on the geography of health should elicit responses that focus on spatial variations in the distribution, causes and impact of ill-health, and the contribution of the environment to patterns of mortality and morbidity.

✔ The view that malnutrition and undernutrition are problems confined to LEDCs is inaccurate. Malnutrition and undernutrition are not uncommon among poor and elderly groups in MEDCs.

✔ Famine impacts different groups in society, hitting the poorest groups with fewest resources and entitlements hardest. Better-off groups may be unaffected by famines.

✔ It is not inevitable that poorer countries have inadequate healthcare systems. Much depends on the quality of governance and government priorities. People can be relatively poor, yet healthy and well educated.

✔ Within rich countries there are spatial differences in mortality and morbidity at both regional and subregional scales.

✔ Within rich countries the quality of healthcare depends partly on where people live and the ease with which they can access healthcare services.

✔ Poor health in rich countries such as the UK is often part of multiple deprivation, and is also associated with poverty, unemployment, poor housing, inadequate education etc.

✔ Poor health is also associated with the most elderly groups. Ageing populations in MEDCs will have huge health implications in the next 20 or 30 years.

9 Geographical skills

Investigative skills

The skills needed in geographical investigation are based on scientific method. This involves asking a research question or testing a hypothesis by collecting data objectively; presenting data in the form of tables, charts and maps; and analysing data, often using statistical techniques. Finally, evaluation of outcomes will determine the validity of the research question or hypothesis.

Identifying a question or hypothesis — Revised

Questions or **hypotheses** should be chosen in the context of a theory or processes. They should also be practicable and feasible to investigate. In a river study based on fieldwork, a legitimate question might be: how does channel efficiency affect channel deposition? As a hypothesis the research question might be re-phrased thus: *as channel width/depth increases there is an increase in channel aggradation*. Formulating a suitable research question or hypothesis is crucial: it provides the framework for the resulting investigation.

A **hypothesis** is a statement about a presumed relationship or difference between variables whose validity is testable using scientific method.

Data collection — Revised

Accessible and appropriate data sources must be identified. **Primary data** are collected either through observations, measurements and interviews in the field, or from documents such as the census, parish records and directories. **Secondary data**, based on published sources such as textbooks and articles or sourced from government agency websites, may also form the basis for an investigation. Most investigations comprise a mix of primary and secondary data. Most primary data comprise **samples** which are collected objectively, using **random**, **systematic** or **stratified** methods.

Data processing, presentation and analysis — Revised

In order to answer a research question or test a hypothesis, data must be organised, processed and analysed. The first task is to arrange data in tables or arrays, to allow their presentation as charts and maps. When presented in visual form trends and patterns in the data become more obvious and make generalisation and description easier. Analysis may be taken a stage further by using descriptive statistics (e.g. measures of central tendency and dispersion) or inferential statistics (e.g. correlation). The latter allow precise measurement of the differences, relationships and trends in data sets, and for sample data provide information on the probability of outcomes occurring by chance.

Conclusions, evaluation

An investigation concludes with a statement of the main findings and an evaluation of the results and methodology. It will assess the extent to which the investigation has achieved its objectives, and suggest possible improvements and scope for further investigation.

Cartographic skills

The main types of statistical maps used in investigative studies are: **choropleth maps, dot maps, proportional symbol maps, isoline maps** and **flow maps**.

Choropleth maps

Choropleth or proportional shading maps show spatial variations in values between areas by colour or shading (see Figure 8.4). They use standardised data such as ratios, percentages and averages. This is because the number of items in any geographic unit is partly a function of its area. Choropleth maps are popular and easy to construct. However, they have a number of weaknesses:

> **Examiner's tip**
>
> It is important to understand when to use a particular mapping technique as well as to understand the strengths and weaknesses of each technique.

- they give no information about the internal distribution of values within areal units

- the areal units (often administrative units) often vary enormously in size and therefore influence the appearance of the map

- abrupt changes in value occur at the boundaries of areal units; these breaks are artificial and are not present in reality

Dot maps

Dot maps show the location of a given quantity of a variable with a dot of constant size. Unlike choropleth maps, dot maps provide information on the distribution of items within areal units. As a result they provide a very effective representation of geographical distributions. But dot maps also have disadvantages:

- they may give a misleading impression of accuracy: rarely is the distribution of items within areal units known with complete accuracy

- in high density areas where dots merge, recovering statistical information may be difficult, while in low density areas dot maps provide minimal information on distributions

Proportional symbol maps

Proportional symbols used for mapping include circles, squares, triangles and bars (see Figure 4.5). The basic principle is that the area of each symbol is proportional to the value it represents. Proportional symbol maps usually show absolute (not standardised) values. Although proportional symbol maps can convey statistical information visually and effectively they, too, have problems:

- it is difficult for the human eye to judge differences in the areas of symbols (e.g. doubling the size of the sides of a square increases the area four times)
- the placement of symbols in small areas may result in overlapping, causing problems of interpretation
- the placement of symbols within areas (usually centrally) is arbitrary, and like choropleth maps, no information is provided on the internal distribution of values.

Isoline maps

Revised

Isolines (also known as isopleths) are lines on maps that join places of equal value. They are used for geographical distributions that have a continuous distribution — for example, surfaces such as relief (contours), rainfall (isohyets) and temperature (isotherms). Their use in human geography includes journey times (isochrones), transport costs (isodapanes) and land values. Isoline maps have two obvious weaknesses:

- because they are derived from point values, there are often several different solutions to fitting isolines
- isolines are often fitted by interpolation, which assumes a constant gradient of change between data points. This assumption introduces inaccuracy with distributions such as population density, which are often highly irregular

Flow maps

Revised

Flow maps show the movement of people, traffic, goods and information between places. Movements are represented as lines proportional in thickness to the volume of flow. Although visually successful, like other statistical maps, flow maps are highly generalised. This is particularly true of **non-routed flow maps**, where flows are shown as straight lines between places. Routed flow maps, which show actual pathways along streets and transport networks overcome this problem to some extent.

Desire line maps simply show connections between places (e.g. origins of shoppers to a market town) with straight lines of constant thickness. They provide no information on flow volumes.

> **Examiner's tip**
>
> Know that all statistical maps are essentially a compromise in terms of their accuracy, detail, visual impact and data retrieval. For instance, an isoline map may trade visual impact for detail and accuracy.

Graphical skills

Statistical data are also represented by charts or graphs. Charts have a greater visual impact than data tables and show patterns and trends with more clarity.

Line, bar and pie charts

Revised

Line charts (see Figure 5.4) are used to show continuous changes in variables in time and space, such as birth and death rates at quarterly intervals, and rental values with distance from a city centre.

Bar charts (see Figure 6.1) comprise a series of rectangles, proportional in area or length to the values they represent. They are often used where data relate to discrete places or units of time (e.g. census population totals recorded at decennial intervals, mean daily discharge of a river recorded at several gauging stations). **Stacked bar charts** provide additional information on two or more data sets by subdividing the bars. For instance, a stacked bar chart representing the total population of England and Wales at decennial intervals could also show the urban and rural population at each date.

Pie charts (see Figure 7.1) are circular graphs divided into segments to show subgroups in a population. They can be used as an alternative to stacked bar charts. They can also be superimposed on maps to provide information on the absolute value of a variable (proportional to the area of the chart), as well as its subdivisions. Thus a district's population total could be represented by the area of the pie chart, while the segments of the chart could provide information on age structure (i.e. 0–14, 15–39, 40–65, 65+ years).

> **Typical mistake**
>
> The application of line charts and bar charts is often confused by students. If data are continuous in time (e.g. river flow) a line chart is appropriate. If data are discrete, for a specific place or time, a bar chart is preferable.

> **Typical mistake**
>
> Pie charts should always start at 12 o'clock and there should be a limit to the number of classes or segments (seven or eight maximum).

Scatter charts and trend lines

Revised

Scatter charts are used to plot two variables, x and y. Variable x is the **independent variable** which causes change in the **dependent variable** y. The independent variable is always plotted on the horizontal (x) axis; the dependent variable (y) on the vertical axis. For example, the length of the growing season (average days per year) for several sites could be plotted on a scatter chart against altitude (metres above sea level). Here, altitude is the independent variable (x) because it influences the dependent variable (y), the length of the growing season. The closer the scatter of points approximates a straight line, the stronger the relationship.

Sometimes scatter charts are plotted with one or both axes having a **logarithmic scale.** This would be appropriate in two situations:

● where the relationship between x and y shows a geometric increase or decrease (e.g. natural increase of population over time). Using a logarithmic scale converts a curvilinear relationship on a scatter chart to a straight line

● where a data set has a huge range of values, causing the scatter of points to become clustered in a small area of the chart (e.g. population and retail services in a region where settlements vary in size from 100 to 1,000,000)

Distributions on scatter charts can be summarised by fitting a trend line to the scatter of points. This can be done either objectively by fitting a statistical 'least squares' regression line, or subjectively 'by eye'. A trend line provides a useful description of the relationship between two variables, and makes it possible to predict one variable (y) from another (x).

Triangular charts and dispersion diagrams

Revised

Triangular charts are used to plot three percentage values whose sum is 100%. Examples include the proportion of a region's workforce in primary, secondary and tertiary activities, and the proportion of sand, silt and clay in a soil. Triangular charts can provide a visual comparison between places, as well as changes through time.

Dispersion diagrams (see Figure 9.1) are single axis charts which show the distribution of values in a data set. They are often used as a guide to dividing a data set into categories prior to plotting a chart or statistical analysis.

Kite and radial diagrams

Kite diagrams are used to show trends in the distribution of plants and animals along a line of transect. In geography this often means a transect through contrasting habitats such as a coastal dune system. Counts of species and/or plant cover are made at regular intervals along a transect (in this example, perpendicular to the shoreline) using **quadrats**. Data for each quadrat are then plotted as a scatter chart, where the x axis is distance along the line of transect. The y axis extends above and below the x axis by an equal amount, to a maximum value of half the highest count. Half the count for each site is then plotted above and below the x axis. Finally the points are joined with straight lines. The result is a series of kite-like shapes whose area is roughly proportional to the counts at each site.

Radial diagrams are useful where a variable has a directional element. Examples include the frequency of wind directions at a weather station, or the orientation of clasts deposited by a glacier or ice sheet. The circumference represents the compass directions and the radial segments show the proportion of time (or number of days a year) that the wind blows from each direction or the proportion (or number) of clasts oriented in a particular direction.

Now test yourself

1 What are primary and secondary data?
2 How does a choropleth map represent spatial distributions?
3 Name three kinds of isoline.
4 What sort of geographical distributions are most effectively represented by isoline maps?
5 Suggest two reasons why you might choose to represent data with a chart rather than a table.
6 Give two examples of data that could be plotted on a triangular graph.

Answers on p. 127

Statistical skills

Statistical analysis is usually the penultimate stage of geographical investigation. There are two types of statistical analysis: **descriptive** and **inferential**.

Descriptive statistics

Data sets may be summarised by two representative numerical values: these are measures of **central tendency** and measures of **dispersion**.

Measures of central tendency

Measures of central tendency represent data sets by a middle value, around which the other values cluster. There are three standard measures of central tendency: the arithmetic **mean** (or average), the **median** and the **principal mode**.

The arithmetic mean is the sum of values in a data set divided by the total number of values. It is the most widely used measure of central tendency. However, the representativeness of the arithmetic mean depends on the nature of the data set. Because the mean weights each value according to its magnitude, very different data sets can have similar arithmetic means.

The median is the middle value in a data set ranked in order of size. Unlike the mean it gives equal weight to each value and is therefore more representative where data sets contain extreme values.

Unit 2 Geographical skills 115

The **principal mode** is the class in a frequency table (or **histogram**) that contains the most values. It is the least useful measure of central tendency because (a) it is a range, rather than a single value, (b) some data sets have more than one modal class.

Measures of dispersion

Measures of central tendency summarise data sets with a single value but tell us nothing about the dispersion of values. Measures of dispersion complement measures of central tendency and give some indication of the spread of values. They include the **range**, **inter-quartile range** and **standard deviation**.

The range is the simplest dispersion measure and is the difference between the highest and lowest values. The inter-quartile range, based on half the values in a data set, is more representative and is used with the median. Data are arranged in rank order and split into four equal parts or **quartiles**. The boundaries of the upper and lower 25% of values are known as the upper quartile and lower quartile, respectively. The inter-quartile range is the difference between the upper and lower quartiles.

The standard deviation or root mean square deviation, is the most useful and most precise measure of dispersion. It is used with the arithmetic mean, and its calculation involves all the values in a data set. Because the standard deviation is strongly influenced by the magnitude of the arithmetic mean, for comparative purposes (e.g. differences in runoff in two drainage basins) we often express the standard deviation as a percentage of the mean. This statistic is called the **coefficient of variation**.

> A **histogram** is a type of bar chart which represents a frequency distribution. Data are divided into class (horizontal axis), each represented by a bar. The frequency of occurrence of values in each class is shown on the vertical axis.

> **Examiner's tip**
>
> Measures of central tendency and dispersion are shorthand summaries of data sets. Be aware of their strengths and weaknesses and the characteristics of data sets to which they are most relevant.

Inferential statistics and statistical significance

Revised

Spearman rank correlation

Correlation measures the statistical association between two variables, x and y, where x is the independent variable and y the dependent variable. For example, correlation could be used in a river study to measure the relationship between channel gradient (x) and flow velocity (y). Correlation analysis yields a **correlation coefficient** that ranges in value from +1 to −1, where +1 is a perfect **positive correlation** (i.e. as x increases there is a proportional increase in y), and −1 is a perfect **negative correlation** (i.e. an increase in x results in a proportional decrease in y). In the example above, we would expect channel gradient and flow velocity to be positively correlated. A correlation close to zero suggests little or no relationship.

Spearman rank correlation is one of a family of correlation measures. Its distinctive feature is that it uses **ordinal** data. In other words the original data, measured on a **ratio** or **interval scale**, are converted to rank values based on their order of magnitude.

Statistical significance

Statistical significance tells us the likelihood that a statistical outcome of an investigation (i.e. the association between variables or the difference between data sets) has occurred by chance. For instance, if our analysis of channel gradient and flow velocity, based on ten sample pairs, produced a correlation coefficient of +0.8, it would suggest a fairly strong association between the two variables. However, the result is still questionable because it is based on a small sample.

> Data measured on a **ratio scale** have a true zero, e.g. a river with a mean discharge of 10 cumecs has twice the flow of a river with a discharge of 5 cumecs.
>
> Data measured on an **interval scale** do not have a true zero, e.g. an air temperature of 20°C does not indicate twice as much heat energy in the atmosphere as a temperature of 10°C.

Therefore, the possibility exists that it could be due to chance. A test for statistical significance enables us to determine this possibility. This is done by referring to significance tables for the Spearman rank correlation coefficient. In this example the tables show that for a sample of 10, a coefficient of +0.65 and above is needed in order to be **95% confident** that the result has not occurred by chance (i.e. to be statistically significant). Thus we can say, with 95% certainty, that an increase in channel gradient causes an increase in flow velocity.

> The **95% confidence** level is the accepted threshold for statistical significance in most geographical investigations.

Now test yourself

Tested ☐

7 Give two reasons why you might use a logarithmic scale on a chart.

8 Give one weakness of the arithmetic mean.

9 Define the terms 'independent' and 'dependent' variable.

10 In what circumstances would you use the coefficient of variation?

11 What is the value of a Spearman rank correlation coefficient for: (a) perfect positive relationships, (b) perfect inverse relationship, (c) no relationship/random?

Check your understanding

1 Draw a diagram to show the main stages followed in geographical investigation.

2 Assess the relative merits of choropleth, dot and isoline for representing population density in a rural area at the county scale.

3 What is the value of measures of central tendency and measures of dispersion?

4 What is meant by 'statistical significance' and why is it important in statistical analysis?

Answers on p. 128

Exam practice

1 With reference to a fieldwork investigation you have undertaken answer the following questions:
   (a) (i) State the hypothesis or research question you investigated and outline one method of sampling you used. [6]
   (ii) Evaluate the advantages and disadvantages of your sampling method. [6]
   (b) Describe one technique you used to present your data. [5]
   (c) Discuss the extent to which the outcome of your investigation was consistent with the theory, concepts or ideas on which it was based. [8]

2 With reference to a fieldwork investigation you have undertaken answer the following questions:
   (a) (i) State the aims and objectives of your investigation. [6]
   (ii) Describe and justify the data collection method(s) that you used. [6]
   (b) Describe one statistical technique you used to analyse your data. [5]
   (c) Outline the main conclusions of your investigation and discuss the extent to which you achieved your aims and objectives. [8]

3 Study the dispersion diagram in Figure 9.1 which shows hydraulic radii for a sample of channel cross-sections at upstream sites on Eglingham Burn. The hydraulic radius is a measure of channel efficiency.

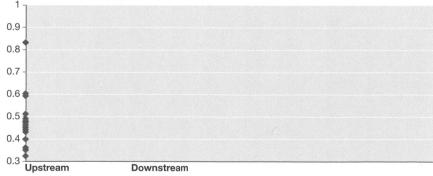

Figure 9.1 Hydraulic radii at upstream and downstream sites: Eglingham Burn

(a) (i) Plot the hydraulic radii values in Table 9.1 for downstream sites. [3]

Table 9.1 Hydraulic radii for downstream sites on Eglingham Burn

0.52	0.79	0.92
0.67	0.73	0.69
0.54	0.82	0.78
0.93	0.70	0.83
0.82	0.58	0.99
0.58	0.74	0.84

(ii) At upstream sites the mean value for the hydraulic radius is 0.48. Calculate the mean value for the hydraulic radius at downstream sites. [3]

(iii) Give possible reasons for the changes in the hydraulic radius between upstream and downstream sites. [4]

(b) Study Figure 9.2 which is a 1:25,000 Ordnance Survey extract covering part of upper Swaledale in North Yorkshire.

(i) Construct a cross-section of the valley of Swinner Beck between points A and B. [4]

(ii) Draw an idealised sketch map showing the relief of the Swinner Beck valley. Add labels to identify the main landforms and annotations to explain the relationships between landforms and processes. [4]

(iii) How and why does the cross-sectional shape of the Swale valley between points C and D differ from the Swinner Beck valley? [6]

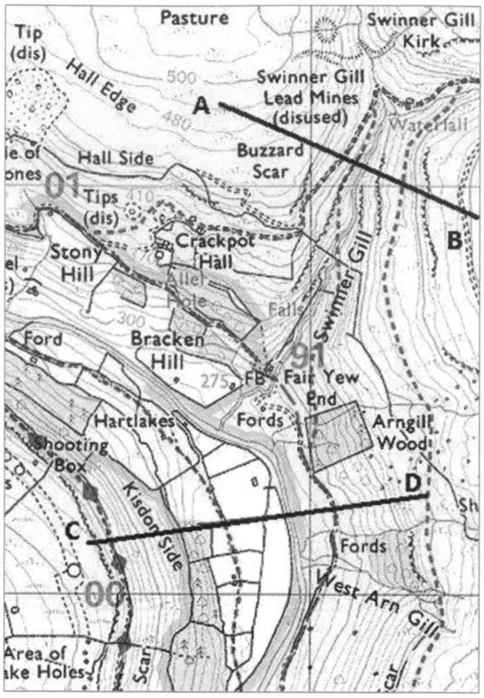

Answers and quick quiz 9 online

Figure 9.2 Ordnance Survey extract
© Ordnance Survey (Licence number 100027418)

Online

Examiner's summary

✔ Students must adopt a logical and systematic approach to geographical enquiry based on scientific method.

✔ The purpose of statistical maps is to present and store spatial numerical data.

✔ Students must have a critical awareness of the strengths and weaknesses of all statistical maps, and realise that they are a compromise between visual effectiveness and clarity, and accuracy and detail.

✔ An evaluation of statistical maps allows students to make reasoned choices of those maps which are most suitable to presenting specific geographical information.

✔ Graphs and charts are effective, visual summaries of generalised data which help to identify broad patterns and trends in data sets.

✔ Statistics allow a deeper, more precise and more objective understanding of the relationships and differences between data sets.

✔ It is important to select appropriate statistical techniques to describe and analyse data sets in geographical investigations.

✔ An understanding of statistical significance is key to the effective use of statistical analysis in geographical investigations.

Answers

Chapter 1

Now test yourself

1. (a) The water balance is where, over time, precipitation inputs to a drainage basin are equal to outputs from evapotranspiration and runoff, and storage. (b) Water is stored in drainage basins by vegetation, soils and porous rocks. Storage delays the throughput of water in the drainage basin and reduces the variability of runoff.

2. River discharge is influenced by: precipitation amounts, precipitation types, evapotranspiration, soil moisture status, geology, land use, slopes etc.

3. Following a precipitation event flashy rivers rise rapidly to a high (but often short-lived) peak flow. Flooding is therefore more sudden and highly unpredictable.

4.
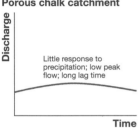
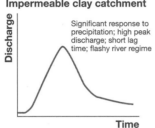

5. (a) Load is the sediment and dissolved minerals transported by a river. (b) Suspended load is silt and clay that is entrained by the flow. It requires relatively high energy (i.e. high water volume, high velocity). Traction load or bedload is large rock particles that slide and roll along the river bed. It requires very high energy levels. Dissolved load is transported continually, whether energy levels are high or low.

6. Bankfull discharge is the maximum flow accommodated by a river channel. Any further increase in flow leads to flooding. A river has maximum energy at bankfull. It can therefore carry the most sediment and effect the most erosion.

7.
V-shaped valley | **Floodplain**

Steep slopes; narrow valley floor; incised valley; interlocking spurs. Vertical incision by river due to steep gradient | Wide, flat valley floor; steep slopes to edge of valley (bluffs). Valley floor filled with alluvium from old channel bars and overbank (flood) deposits. Gentle channel gradient. Lateral erosion, with channel shifting across flood plain and widening valley where channel meets bluffs.

8. Floodplains are formed by erosion and deposition. As the meandering river shifts its channel across the valley floor, lateral erosion widens the valley where it engages the valley edge (bluff). The valley floor is filled with alluvium by (a) flooding — fine suspended load, (b) old abandoned channel bars (coarser sands and pebbles).

9.
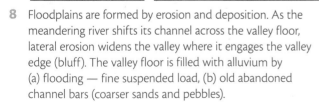
Efficient channel: large cross-sectional area; small wetted perimeter. Little energy loss to friction. | Inefficient channel: small cross-sectional area; large wetted perimeter. Much energy dissipated as friction.

10. Rivers have braided channels because of: very high sediment loads, coarse sediment loads, incoherent banks, steep channel gradients, extreme variations in discharge.

11.
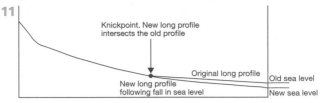

12. Physical causes of river floods: excessive (high intensity or prolonged) precipitation, high antecedent moisture, rapid snowmelt; human causes: deforestation, urbanisation, land drainage.

13. Exposure is the magnitude and frequency of flood events; vulnerability is the preparedness in the face of flood risks and the distribution of the population in relation to flood-prone areas.

14. (a) Flash floods are caused by rapid runoff in response to intense precipitation events (e.g. thunderstorms). They are most common in summer. Steep slopes, impermeable catchments, deforestation etc. contribute to flash floods. (b) Slow floods result from heavy and prolonged precipitation (most often in winter), sometimes over several weeks.

15. Hard engineering: dam construction, levee building. Soft engineering: reafforestation of headwaters, floodplain management.

16. Soft engineering causes less damage to the environment, is economically sustainable and has a lower cost.

Check your understanding

1. Hjulström's curve and erosion: sand-sized particles are eroded and transported at relatively low flow velocities, large particles (e.g. pebbles, cobbles) and very fine particles (clay) are only transported at high velocities. Deposition: a slight reduction in flow velocity causes coarse particles to stop moving; further reduction results in the deposition of sand; and fine particles fall out of suspension at the slowest velocities. The outcome is that coarse sediments are transported relatively short distances while fine particles, once entrained, may be transported hundreds of kilometres.

2. Severn Valley flood: widespread flooding around Tewkesbury and Gloucester with damage to property and disruption of businesses; households left without power and water; motorists stranded on the M5 by floodwaters; crops submerged and maize, potatoes and hay crops destroyed; insured losses were estimated at between £1 and £1.5 billion. Indus Valley flood: c. 2,000 deaths and 1.2 million homes destroyed; 10 million people displaced and 8 million needed emergency relief aid; shortages of food, clean drinking water; inadequate sanitation; water-borne diseases such as cholera and diarrhoea; economic costs, estimated between $3.5 and $5 billion; Pakistan's GDP was forecast to fall by 2% in 2011; massive damage to physical infrastructure and agriculture.

3. LEDCs are more vulnerable to flood hazards because there are fewer flood protection/management structures, poverty means that flood victims have fewer resources to cope with flood disasters, poor infrastructure makes it difficult to distribute disaster relief, poverty forces millions to live in flood-prone areas.

4

	Hard engineering	Soft engineering
Human	People displaced by dams, reservoirs; villages flooded.	Relocation of populations away from floodplains. Problems of getting agreement to land use change from owners.
Environmental	Rivers isolated from floodplains; drainage of wetlands and loss of habitat; impact on aquatic ecosystems and wildlife; sustainability.	Modification of habitats through reafforestation programmes. Will not eliminate floods and give complete flood protection.
Economic	High cost of dams, levees, etc. High cost of maintenance.	Cost of relocating business and populations away from floodplains.

Chapter 2

Now test yourself

1 The accumulation zone is the area above the snowline where annual accumulation of snow exceeds ablation. The ablation zone is the zone where annual melting and loss of snow/ice exceeds annual accumulation. The equilibrium line is the place on a glacier where there is an annual balance between accumulation and ablation.

2

Glacier advances **Glacier retreats**

Input snow Output snow

3 Warm-based glaciers are those where the temperature of the ice interface with the ground is above freezing. Cold-based glaciers are those where the interface temperature is below freezing. Warm-based glaciers move rapidly and are effective agents of erosion. Cold-based glaciers are frozen to the ground surface and protect, rather than erode, the ground.

4 Glaciers move by basal sliding and by internal deformation.

5 A freeze–thaw cycle occurs when temperatures during a 24 hour period fluctuate above and below freezing. They control rates of physical weathering because when water freezes its volume expands by 9%. As a result rocks are stressed and break down by frost action.

6 Abrasion is the scouring action of rock particles dragged across the ground surface by a glacier. Plucking/quarrying is where glacier ice freezes onto rock surfaces and removes them as the glacier moves under gravity.

7 Landforms of alpine glaciation: arêtes, pyramidal peaks, cirques, U-shaped valleys, hanging valleys, truncated spurs, ribbon lakes.

8 A valley glacier is a tongue of glacier ice, confined by the steep walls of a valley. An ice sheet is a vast expanse of ice, sometimes several kilometres thick, which blankets the landscape (the highest peaks — nunataks — may emerge above the ice sheet).

9 Moraines are rock debris transported by glaciers and deposited when the ice melts. Fluvio-glacial deposits are rock debris transported and deposited by meltwater streams. Fluvio-glacial deposits are sorted; moraines are unsorted.

10 A drumlin is a low, streamlined hill deposited and shaped by a moving ice sheet. A terminal moraine is debris dumped by a glacier at its snout/leading edge, often associated with stagnant ice. An esker is a long sinuous ridge formed from the channel deposits of a meltwater stream. An outwash plain is an extensive area of fluvio-glacial deposits beyond an ice front.

11 A glacial environment is an environment covered or partly covered by glaciers and ice sheets. A periglacial environment is a cold environment supporting permafrost but free of ice cover.

12 Permafrost is perennially frozen ground. The active layer is the uppermost layer of regolith in periglacial environments which thaws during the summer. Talik is an area of unfrozen ground, surrounded by permafrost.

13 A pingo is a small, ice-cored hill.

14 Solifluction mantles the landscape in a thick and extensive layer of regolith (rock debris). It produces low-angled landscapes with little variation in relief.

15 The permafrost is maintained only by a delicate thermal balance, biodiversity is low, food chains are short. Recovery from damage to climate and ecosystems is slow and uncertain.

Check your understanding

1 Glacier budget (or mass balance) is the annual difference between inputs of fresh snow and loss of snow and ice to ablation. During a period of higher snowfall or lower temperatures the glacier budget becomes positive, which causes glaciers to increase in volume and advance. The reverse situation will result in glacier retreat. There may be a considerable time lag between changes in a glacier's budget and its response.

2

	Origin			Type	
Landform	G	F	W	E	D
Corrie, arête	✓		✓	✓	
U-shaped valley	✓			✓	
Hanging valley truncated spur	✓			✓	
Terminal, lateral, recessional moraine	✓				✓
Drumlin	✓				✓
Esker, kame		✓			✓
Outwash plain		✓			✓
Meltwater channel		✓		✓	

Origin: **G** = Glacial, **F** = Fluvio-glacial, **W** = Weathering.
Type: **E** = Erosional, **D** = Depositional

3 Cold environments are fragile, easily degraded and are slow to recover from environmental damage. The development of arctic oil and gas reserves has damaging environmental effects: oil spillages, melting permafrost, roads, disruption of

migrating caribou herds, noise, pollution of rivers. But steps are taken by energy companies and governments to minimise the environmental impact: permafrost is insulated, engineering work confined to winter months before the active layer thaws, human waste removed, creation of conservation/wilderness areas.

4 Indigenous populations in the Arctic and sub-Arctic are either hunters or livestock herders. Inuit people living in northern Canada and Alaska hunt fish, seals, walruses, whales, birds, caribou etc. and collect fruits during the brief arctic summer. The economy of the Sami of northern Scandinavia and northern Russia is based on semi-domesticated reindeer herds.

5 The main development pressures in Antarctica are: tourism, overfishing, offshore drilling for oil and gas. Antarctica is protected by international treaty against development, mineral/energy extraction on the continent is forbidden (Antarctica is reserved for scientific research), hazardous substances are banned, discharge of pollutants in Antarctic seas is illegal, fish stocks in the Southern Ocean are managed to create a sustainable fishery.

Chapter 3

Now test yourself

1 Energy inputs to the coastal system are waves, tides, winds.

2 The main coastal erosional processes are: abrasion/corrasion, hydraulic action/quarrying, corrosion.

3 Abrasion erodes a notch at the cliff base, undermining the cliff and ultimately causing collapse. Hydraulic action weakens cliffs in the inter-tidal zone along joints, causing rockfall, cave formation etc. Corrosion dissolves carbonate rocks (limestone, chalk).

4
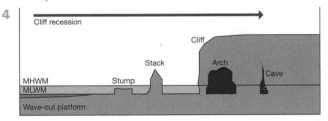

5 A sediment cell is a stretch of coastline in which sediments (sand, shingle) are largely confined, with no total sediment gain from or loss to adjacent cells.

6 Swash alignment occurs when waves are fully refracted and waves break parallel to the shore. Sediments therefore move perpendicular to the shoreline. Drift alignment occurs when waves are not fully refracted and therefore break obliquely to the shoreline. The result is that sediments are transported transversely along the coast.

7 A spit is a drift-aligned beach, joined to the mainland at one (proximal) end. It grows out from the coast across a bay or estuary as a result of longshore drift. Recurves indicate stages in the growth of the spit. The recurves result from the refraction of waves around the far (distal) end of the spit.

8 High percolation rates on coarse shingle limit the extent of the swash zone and reduce the power of the backwash. This results in shingle beaches having a steeper gradient and narrower planforms than sand beaches.

9 Vegetation lowers wind speeds near the surface which causes sand deposition. Growth is stimulated when plants (e.g. marram grass) adapted to dune environments are submerged by sand. This leads to further sand deposition and the development of dunes.

10 (a) A dune slack is a low-lying, waterlogged area between two dune ridges, where the water table reaches the surface. (b) A blow-out is a rapid localised erosion of a sand dune caused by destruction of the vegetation cover (often by human activity).

11 Salt marsh develops from the colonisation of mudflats by vegetation. The vegetation slows the movement of tidal currents, and promotes deposition (sedimentation). Slowly this process builds up the surface of the mudflat, leading to the formation of salt marshes which are only inundated at high tide.

12 *Spartina* (cord grass), *Salicornia* (glasswort) are salt marsh pioneer species.

13 (a) Eustatic change is a worldwide change in sea level caused by an absolute increase or decrease in the volume of water in the oceans. (b) Isostatic change is a localised, relative change in sea level associated with either loading or unloading of the land with ice.

14 (a) A marine transgression is due to eustatic rise in sea level. It floods the coast and causes the coastline to retreat inland. (b) A marine regression is the result of a eustatic fall in sea level. The coastline extends seawards.

15 Coastal squeeze occurs where sea walls/embankments prevent mudflats and salt marshes retreating inland in the face of rising sea levels (associated with global warming). This leads to accelerated erosion of mudflats and salt marshes.

16 Shoreline Management Plan strategies: (1) hold the line, (2) no active intervention (i.e. do nothing), (3) managed realignment.

Check your understanding

1 Sea level rise increases the area over which wave and tidal processes operate. This is likely to intensify erosion and rates of cliff retreat. Where depositional landforms such as dunes, mudflats and salt marshes cannot retreat inland (e.g. steep coastal slopes, sea walls etc.) they will be destroyed by erosion.

2 Erosional landforms develop where: (1) rocks are coherent, resistant to erosion and form steep, stable slopes; (2) the coast has strong relief and is several tens of metres or more above sea level; (3) waves are powerful (i.e. long fetch); (4) sea bed gradients in the nearshore zone are steep so that wave energy is not dissipated before reaching the shore.

3 Coastal dunes owe their formation to the interaction of wind and plants. Plants slow wind speeds near the ground. The resultant loss of energy causes the deposition of sand around plants such as marram grass and sea couch grass. These specialised plants grow rapidly when buried by sand and this promotes further sand deposition and the growth of dunes. On mudflats, pioneer colonisers such as glasswort slow tidal currents and encourage silt and clay deposition. Gradually the height of the mudflats increases, reducing the period of inundation at high tide. This allows colonisation by species less tolerant to inundation and high salt levels until a fully vegetated marsh forms, which is inundated either for a few hours on each tidal cycle or only occasionally on spring tides.

4

	Origin					Type	
Landform	**Wa**	**Wi**	**T**	**B**	**We**	**E**	**D**
Dunes		✓	✓				✓
Salt marsh		✓					✓
Beaches	✓						✓
Cliffs		✓			✓	✓	
Arches, caves, stacks		✓			✓	✓	
Wave-cut platforms		✓		✓		✓	

Origin: **Wa** = Waves, **Wi** = Wind, **T** = Tide, **B** = Biological, **We** = Weathering. Type: **E** = Erosion, **D** = Deposition.

5 Hard engineering responses to coastal erosion and coastal flooding: sea walls, earth/clay embankments, armour blocks (rip rap), revetments, gabions, groynes. Sea walls and embankments protect coastal areas from flooding. Sea walls and other hard engineering structures protect against erosion. Hard coastal defences can be evaluated against several criteria: effectiveness, cost, environmental impact, sustainability.

Chapter 4

Now test yourself

1 Aridity is defined by the ratio of mean annual precipitation to mean annual evapotranspiration.

2 Factors determining rainfall effectiveness: intensity of rainfall, seasonality of rainfall, rates of evapotranspiration, soil porosity.

3 Factors influencing the location of hot deserts: location on the poleward limb of the Hadley Cell (i.e. general circulation), mountain barriers (rain shadows), cold ocean currents.

4

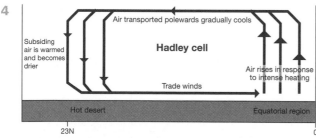

5 Cold ocean currents create temperature inversions (i.e. air is cooler near the surface than aloft). As a result, air near the surface is stable (i.e. it cannot rise freely) and form clouds and precipitation.

6 Mountain ranges block moisture-bearing winds. They also force air aloft, which results in cloud and precipitation over the mountains. Air reaching the leeward side of mountains therefore contains less moisture. In addition, air descending on leeward slopes to lower ground is warmed by compression, making cloud formation and precipitation even less likely. This dry area to the lee of mountain ranges is known as a rain shadow.

7 The main weathering processes in hot deserts and their margins are: salt weathering, insolation weathering and freeze–thaw weathering.

8 Wind erosion is the abrasive effect of sand grains close to the desert surface; deflation is the removal of fine material by wind. Wind transport is the saltation and creep of sand grains; the entrainment in the atmosphere of fine particles (clay and silt).

9 Sand creep is the sliding and rolling of sand particles along the ground caused by the wind. Saltation is the skipping motion of sand particles within a metre or so of the ground surface. As the saltated particles hit the ground they set in motion other particles. In dust storms tiny particles are picked up by the wind and suspended in the atmosphere. Wind speed determines the type of transport and the distances over which particles are transported (i.e. low velocity = creep; moderate velocity = saltation; high velocity = suspension).

10 (a) Yardangs are an erosional desert landform. They are streamlined ridges of solid rock, up to 100 m high, aligned in the direction of the prevailing wind. They are often undercut at the base by abrasive saltating sand grains. (b) Barchans are a type of crescentic dune formed by sand deposition. In planform they are wider than they are long, with steep slip faces on their concave side and horns that face downwind. They are highly mobile and develop where winds blow predominantly from one direction.

11 Desert environments are fragile because of: low biodiversity, highly specialised plant and animal species with sparse populations, slow growth of plants due to aridity and excessive heat, short food chains, soils easily eroded by wind and water if vegetation cover is damaged.

12 Desertification is the degradation of formerly productive land to the point where desert-like conditions prevail.

13 Desertification may be caused by overgrazing. Overgrazing destroys the vegetation cover, exposing the soil to wind and water erosion. Soil erosion reduces the soil's moisture-holding capacity and soil depth, increases runoff and prevents plants recolonising degraded areas. Desertification may also result from prolonged drought.

14 Desertification's adverse effects on farming resources: reduction in water supplies, salinisation of soils (caused by excessive irrigation), destruction of soils following overgrazing/woodland clearance.

15 Salinised fields can be underdrained to lower the water table and prevent salt accumulation at the surface. Shelterbelts can be planted to stabilise soils and prevent further wind erosion.

16 Sustainable farming in desert and semi-desert areas can be achieved by integrating crop cultivation and livestock herding (e.g. in the western Sahel). Crops are rotated and livestock grazing on the open range is controlled. Minimal disturbance of the soil during cultivation reduces water loss by evaporation. Livestock graze on croplands to ensure that nutrients are recycled and crop residues are used for forage.

Check your understanding

1 Plants have adapted to low rainfall and drought by: storing water in leaves and stems, reducing moisture loss by modifying leaves, developing long roots, evading drought by completing life cycles in the few weeks that follow rain, remaining dormant until rain falls.

2 Water is an effective geomorphological agent in deserts because: (a) there is little vegetation; (b) regolith covers large areas and is loose and unconsolidated; (c) ephemeral streams and rivers following thunderstorms have high energy; (d) slopes are often steep, especially in rocky deserts. Landforms associated with water erosion and deposition include: alluvial fans, bajadas, playas, canyons and pediments.

3

	Origin		Type	
Landform	**Wi**	**Wa**	**E**	**D**
Dunes	✓			✓
Yardangs, zeugens	✓		✓	
Deflation hollows	✓		✓	
Alluvial fans/bajadas		✓		✓
Playas		✓		✓
Canyons		✓	✓	
Pediments		✓	✓	

Origin: **Wi** = Wind, **Wa** = Water. Type: **E** = Erosional, **D** = Depositional.

4

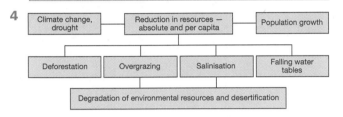

Chapter 5

Now test yourself

1 Vital rates are crude birth rates and crude death rates.

2 Population change in a city or region = births – deaths ± migration.

3 The crude birth rate (CBR) is strongly affected by age structure. Birth rates are relatively high in countries or societies with a large proportion of young adults. An aged population structure produces relatively low birth rates. The CBR is not an accurate indicator of fertility, i.e. average number of children born to each woman in a country.

4 Life expectancy is the average life span of an individual at birth. Migration is the permanent movement of a person or population to a new place of residence (usually at a regional or international scale). Net migrational change is the annual difference between in-migrants and out-migrants to a country or region.

5

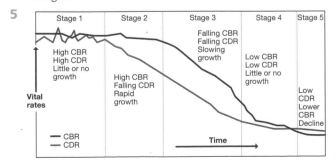

6

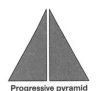

Progressive pyramid   Regressive pyramid

7 Migration is selective in terms of age, gender and education.

8 An ageing population is one where the average age of its members increases, either because people are living longer (reduction in mortality) or there has been a decline in fertility (a smaller proportion of children and young people in the population). The economic implications are increased dependency with a smaller proportion of economically active adults and a larger proportion of older people. This has implications for economic growth (lower GDP per capita) and a larger proportion of spending on healthcare and pensions for the elderly.

9 Migration is selective and mainly involves young adults. (a) In rural areas this results in an ageing population and a rising proportion of old people. (b) In urban areas migrants often have young families or, because they are young, are likely to produce children. The result is an increasing proportion of children who are dependent on economically active adults.

10 Pro-natalist population policies promote fertility (e.g. tax benefits to families with children, free schooling, free healthcare). Anti-natalist policies aim to reduce fertility by supporting birth control and family planning. In free democratic counties population policies rely on incentives and persuasion. In authoritarian societies citizens may be coerced or pressured into having fewer or more children.

11 Rapid urban growth in LEDCs often results in: makeshift/slum housing, lack of essential services (electricity, clean water, sanitation, roads, schools etc.), lack of employment, degraded urban environment and disease.

12 Problems caused by counterurbanisation in rural areas: unaffordable housing for rural populations, loss of services (public transport, shops), building on greenfield sites, increased traffic, loss of social community/cohesion in villages.

13 Rural depopulation in MEDCs affects rural services provision by: undermining thresholds (because of population decline) and making the provision of many services unprofitable, ageing of populations (fewer young adults and therefore fewer children) and the resulting closure of primary schools.

14 Segregation of ethnic minorities may be due to one or more of the following: cheap housing (ethnic minorities often have lower incomes than other groups), the availability of ethnic services (mosques, temples, ethnic food shops), attraction of people of similar culture (common language and traditions), discrimination by the host society and the need for security.

15 Multiple deprivation has several dimensions: low income, unemployment, poor housing, poor education, ill-health, vulnerability to crime/anti-social behaviour, etc.

16 Multiple deprivation limits the full participation of individuals and socio-economic groups in society. Low income and unemployment prevents access to decent housing in crime-free areas served by good state schools. Poor housing and low income may affect diet, mental health and physical wellbeing, further limiting an individual's prospects and ability to play any meaningful role in society.

Check your understanding

1 Governments adopt various strategies to manage population change. Anti-natalist strategies aim to stabilise (or even reduce) total numbers through the promotion of family planning, the availability of abortion or restrictions imposed on family size. The motive is usually economic. Pro-natalist strategies aim to increase a population, either for economic, cultural and political reasons. Financial incentives, tax breaks and the banning of artificial contraceptives are designed to increase fertility. Governments also target international immigration, encouraging immigration of young adult and skilled workers to provide a quick fix for a country's economic problems.

2 Social impact of an ageing population: increase in the number of single-person households, increased incidence of disability (mental and physical) and demands on carers, problems of mobility and access to services. Economic impact: increase in dependency, increasing proportion of GDP directed to pensions and healthcare/social services.

3 Social impact of rapid population growth in cities in LEDCs: overcrowding, disease, families with one parent, poor educational opportunities, poor housing. Environmental impact: inadequate sanitation, little or no refuse disposal, polluted rivers (and polluted drinking water), atmospheric pollution (domestic fires, cooking stoves etc.).

4 Rural depopulation is the absolute decrease in the population of a rural area, caused by either net migrational loss or low birth rates and high death rates or a combination of both. The main implication of depopulation is a loss of rural services. Demand falls as populations decline, and services such as shops, post offices, GPs, public transport etc. are withdrawn. Because out-migration is age-selective, ageing of rural populations is common in MEDCs, and primary schools are closed.

Chapter 6

Now test yourself

1 Regions of food surplus: North America, South America. Regions of food deficit: Europe, Africa, Asia.

2 Factors influencing the scale of food production: area of farmland, physical conditions for farming (relief, soil, climate), technology, capital, level of domestic demand.

3 Increase in world food prices is due to: increased demand from Asia, world population growth, poor harvests, increased price of oil/fertiliser, diversion of farmland from food crops to biofuels, trade restrictions.

4 Trade blocs influence the global trade in food by: import tariffs, export subsidies, crop subsidies paid to producers.

5
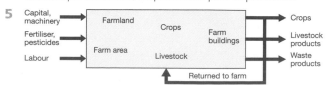

6 Commercial farming systems are geared towards profit-making and selling production for cash. Subsistence farming systems are largely non-commercial, with most crops consumed on the farm and not exchanged for cash.

7 Intensive farming systems: wet rice cultivation, horticulture, irrigation agriculture. Extensive farming systems: hill sheep farming, nomadic pastoralism.

8 The Green Revolution was a largely successful attempt to increase cereal production in LEDCs in the 1970s by cultivating new high-yielding varieties of rice and wheat. It relied on inputs of chemical fertilisers, pesticides and irrigation water.

9

Advantages	Disadvantages
Higher crop yields.	Only benefited a minority of better-off farmers; increased inequality.
Higher incomes for farmers.	Most farmers could not afford agro-chemical inputs.
Greatly increased outputs of cereals so that countries such as India no longer had to rely on staple food imports.	Minimal benefit to farmers without access to irrigation.
Increased demand for rural labour.	In order to pay for agro-chemicals many women became farm labourers, forcing down agricultural wages.
	High-yielding varieties prone to disease. Farmers have to buy costly pesticides.

10 GM crops are controversial because their impact on the natural environment (and human health) is not fully understood and could be harmful.

11 Amazonia is unsuited to permanent, settled cultivation. Soils are leached and impoverished. Sustainable cultivation is only possible through a type of shifting agriculture with long periods of fallow. Low-intensity cattle farming and plantation crops (e.g. coffee) are the only sustainable types of modern agriculture.

12 The commercialisation of agriculture is the development of a more market-based approach to farming among subsistence and quasi-subsistence farmers. Production becomes increasingly centred on cash crops sold in regional, national and international markets.

13 Advantages of intermediate technology to farmers: low cost, relies on local and traditional skills, uses local resources, sustainable (both economically and environmentally).

14 EU strategies to ensure food security: price support to farmers for some crops, price support to farmers in less favoured areas (e.g. uplands), external tariff to prevent cheap foreign food competition with EU farmers, subsidies for food exports to give EU farmers an advantage in foreign markets. Environmental policies of EU and UK include: cross-compliance to qualify for subsidies, Environmental Stewardship, Environmentally Sensitive Areas.

15 Arguments for high-value crops (fruit, vegetables, flowers): many small farmers benefit — higher incomes; provides employment — labour intensive farming; high-value crops suffer less from price fluctuations than traditional cash crops such as coffee and cocoa. Arguments against: many small farmers cannot meet the standardisation and quality requirements of supermarkets; good quality land taken for export crops rather than staple food crops for local people; large carbon footprint because of reliance on air transport (air miles).

16 (a) Organic farming is the production of crops without the use of agro-chemicals and drugs and antibiotics used in commercial livestock farming. (b) Agribusiness is large-scale, capital-intensive farming. Unlike family farms, agribusiness is owned and controlled by large businesses and employs specialist farm managers.

17 Arguments in favour of locally grown food: shorter supply chains therefore less transport and greener; provides local employment; supports small, family-run farms.

18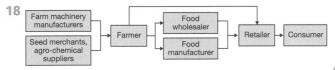

19 A TNC is a large international company that in the food industry is involved in sourcing, growing, manufacturing and marketing food worldwide. Examples of TNCs in the food industry are Coca Cola, Nestle, Chiquita, McDonald's.

Check your understanding

1 Food insecurity — often connected to global food shortages and rising prices — may result in trade restrictions on food imports and exports. External tariffs (e.g. in the EU) protect farmers from competition from cheaper food imports and help to secure domestic food supplies. Government concerns about climate change have led to the replacement of food crops with biofuels. This has created food shortages and has inflated cereal prices. Some Middle East governments and China lease large areas of arable land overseas to secure food supplies.

2 Arable farming in many MEDCs is practised as agribusiness. Its main features are: farms covering thousands of hectares; large-scale use of machinery (tractors, combines, grain dryers etc.); high inputs of agro-chemicals; long-term contracts with food manufacturers and supermarkets; professional farm managers. In many LEDCs in Asia and Africa arable farming has different characteristics: small-scale family farms/smallholdings; labour intensive; high yields per hectare; use of organic fertiliser (often in short supply); some integration of livestock and crop farming; subsistence or quasi-subsistence rather than commercial.

3 Food production in LEDCs could be increased by: application of new technologies; intensifying existing farm systems; developing more sustainable farm systems; extending production into new (unfarmed) areas. New technologies include the wider application of innovations such as the Green Revolution, and genetic modification (GM) of crops. Both are capital intensive and may be inappropriate for small peasant farms. Those farmers able to benefit from Green Revolution technology may be a small minority. The long-term effects of GM are unknown. Extending irrigation could benefit millions of farmers. Intensification is likely to mean greater inputs of agro-chemicals, which may be beyond the means of farmers. It may also result in environmental degradation (e.g. overgrazing,

overcultivation). More sustainable farming, integrating arable farming with livestock and sylviculture, is possible but requires changes in traditional farming methods and education of farmers. The scope for extending the cultivated area is limited. It often results in the replacement of forest and woodland with arable land. This is environmentally damaging and may be unsustainable (e.g. clearance of rainforest in Brazil for cultivation and grazing).

4 Since the 1960s, the CAP has secured supplies of basic foods (e.g. cereals, dairy products, sugar beet, oilseed) in the EU. But in the 1970s and 1980s EU subsidies led to massive overproduction (production outstripped demand) and environmental degradation. In the past 20 years the CAP has been more successful. Food production is roughly in line with demand and farming has responded to incentives and controls to protect the environment.

Chapter 7

Now test yourself

1 Renewables: HEP, solar, geothermal, wind, wave, tidal, biofuels. Non-renewables: oil, coal, natural gas, nuclear. Recyclable: HEP, biofuels, nuclear. Inexhaustible: solar, geothermal, wind, wave, tidal.

2 Disadvantages of fossil fuels: finite resources; pollute the atmosphere, contributing to global warming, climate change and acid rain.

3 Primary energy is energy that is consumed directly, e.g. burning oil for transport, gas for space heating. Secondary energy involves the conversion of primary energy to electricity, e.g. burning coal to drive turbines and generators to produce electric power.

4 Coal producers: China, USA, Australia; consumers: China, USA, India. Oil producers: Russia, Saudi Arabia, USA; consumers: USA, China, Japan. Gas producers: USA, Russia, Canada; consumers: USA, Russia, Iran.

5 Main trends in global energy patterns over the last 30 years have been increases in the total amount of energy produced and consumed; increase in the proportion of energy derived from renewables and nuclear; rapid increase in energy consumption in Asia, especially China and India; big increase in natural gas consumption, lower rates of increase for coal and oil.

6 Energy cartels such as OPEC influence oil production and therefore play a key role in determining prices; conflicts in the Middle East (e.g. Libya 2011, Iraq 2003) threaten oil supplies and inflate prices; TNCs influence supplies through investment decisions, accidents (e.g. spillages).

7 Pipelines are particularly vulnerable, crossing international boundaries and sometimes extending for thousands of kilometres (easy targets for terrorists or in political conflicts); several oil tanker routes pass close to countries which harbour terrorists (e.g. Yemen, Somalia); a large proportion of oil and gas exports originate in the Middle East, geopolitically a highly unstable region.

8

	Adverse environmental effects.
Renewables	HEP — flooding of valleys/damage to river ecology/siltation.
	Wind — threat to birds, visual intrusion, noise pollution.
	Tidal — damage to salt water ecosystems, loss of habitat for birds, fish, molluscs, shellfish.
Non-renewables	Coal — acid rain, GHG emissions, air pollution, spoil heaps, subsidence.
	Oil — oil spills, GHG emissions.
	Gas — GHG emissions.
	Nuclear — accidents/leaks of radioactive materials to environment.

9

Arguments for nuclear energy	Arguments against nuclear energy
Does not contribute to GHG emissions, global warming and climate change.	Threat to human populations and the environment as a result of accidents/radioactive leaks.
Energy security (availability of uranium from politically stable countries).	Radioactive pollution can persist for hundreds of years.
Diversifies energy production.	No permanent storage yet for spent and reprocessed nuclear fuel.
Only three major accidents in 30+ years (Three Mile Island, Chernobyl, Fukushima).	Risk of terrorist attack.
	Difficult to find remote sites for power stations in small, densely populated countries.

10 Causes of acid rain:
- Sulphur dioxide emissions from coal-burning power stations.
- Vehicle exhaust gases (nitrogen oxide).
- Ammonia from agriculture.

Consequences of acid rain:
- Destruction of forests through wet and dry deposition.
- Damage to soils and release of toxic metals, e.g. aluminium.
- Pollution of lakes and watercourse leading to death of aquatic life.

11 (a) Renewable energy is energy from sources that are either recyclable or inexhaustible (e.g. HEP); sustainable energy is energy that can be produced without causing long-term environmental damage (e.g. solar). (b) Carbon-free energy is energy production that does not result in CO_2 emissions (e.g. nuclear); carbon neutral energy is energy production where there is a balance between the release of CO_2 and its absorption by plants in photosynthesis (e.g. biofuels).

12 Fossil fuels are finite resources: once used they cannot be replaced (except on timescales measured in millions of years).

13 The environmental advantages of renewables: renewable energy is infinite — either recyclable (e.g. biofuels) or inexhaustible (e.g. solar power); renewable energy does not produce GHGs (responsible for global warming) nor sulphur dioxide and nitrogen oxide (the causes of acid rain).

14 The environmental disadvantages of renewables: dams constructed for HEP flood large areas and damage aquatic ecosystems; tidal barrages destroy salt-water, estuarine ecosystems; wind turbines are visually intrusive, noisy and kill wild birds; offshore wind turbines may damage/disrupt marine ecosystems, while onshore, the location of wind farms in uplands may damage sensitive environments (e.g. peat bogs); the construction of renewable hardware involves large emissions of GHGs.

Check your understanding

1 A country's energy mix is influenced by: its domestic energy resources; accessing secure energy supplies; diversification to avoid excessive dependence on a narrow range of fuels; environmental considerations — reducing GHG emissions; political considerations (e.g. public distrust of nuclear power).

2 A large proportion of the crude oil that enters world trade originates in the Middle East. This is a politically unstable region (numerous conflicts, coups and revolutions in the past 30 years) which affects world oil supplies, prices and energy security for major oil importers. Given the value of oil to the world economy, regions such as the Arabian peninsula, Persian Gulf and North Africa have great strategic importance. The result is close political and military involvement in Middle Eastern affairs by western powers.

3

	Coal	Nuclear
Energy security	Mainly indigenous therefore a reliable energy resource; limited international trade in coal. Coal reserves will last at least 200 years at present rates of consumption.	Fairly reliable sources of uranium (main suppliers are politically stable countries). Uranium reserves sufficient to last for 50 years or so — longer if spent fuel is reprocessed.
Environmental	Accidents at coal-fired power stations cause minimal environmental damage. New technologies (e.g. carbon capture) may solve problems of GHG emissions in future.	No GHG emissions, therefore a clean source of energy that does not contribute to global warming and climate change.
Economic	Relatively cheap; produces electricity at low-cost.	Uranium prices less volatile than oil and gas; quantities of uranium consumed only a tiny fraction of fossil fuels.

4 The UK needs a diversified energy budget without excessive reliance on just one or two energy sources; nuclear is 'clean' and does not contribute to global warming, climate change, acid rain (UK has international environmental obligations); supplies of uranium are assured in the medium-term; nuclear is safe — only one major accident in the UK in 1957; the nuclear industry is already a significant employer — further investment will safeguard jobs.

5 The energy gap is the shortfall in electricity production that will occur in the UK in the next 10 years as existing nuclear power stations are decommissioned (most are over 40 years old). If energy demand is to be met, investment is needed in new capacity. The UK government gave the go-ahead in 2009 to fill the energy gap by building ten new nuclear power stations. The first should be ready by 2018.

Chapter 8

Now test yourself

1 (a) Mortality is the incidence of death (at a given age); morbidity is ill-health that limits a person's lifestyle/economic activity. (b) Life expectancy is the average number of years an individual can expect to live at birth, or at a given age; healthy life expectancy is the number of years an individual can expect to live in good health.

2

Demographic impact of HIV/ AIDS	Economic impact of HIV/AIDS
• Changes in total population over time: (slowing, static, decline). • Reduction in the proportion of younger adults in the population. • Reduction in the proportion of children in the population. • Households with only one or no adults (orphaned children).	• Greater demands on healthcare services. • Lower productivity from workers: economic output falls. • Poverty in families most affected by disease.

3 Diabetes is a disease of affluence related to lifestyle. It is linked to high-fat calorie-rich diets, lack of exercise and obesity.

4 Malnutrition is a lack of adequate nutrition caused by an unbalanced diet (usually insufficient protein and lack of essential vitamins).

5 Undernutrition describes insufficient food (calorie) intake to maintain good health.

6 Two causes of obesity are: excessive consumption of high energy foods; lack of physical exercise.

7 Famine impacts most on the poorest members of society who have the fewest resources and entitlements to purchase food.

8 TNCs can adversely affect human health by: promoting unhealthy products/foods (e.g. tobacco, fast food), failing to develop drugs to protect populations in poor countries from disease, manufacturing processes causing environmental pollution.

9 Poorer regions/districts of the UK suffer higher rates of morbidity and mortality from cancer, heart disease, respiratory disease, alcohol abuse etc. Thus northern Britain has higher morbidity and mortality than southern Britain. Within cities, rich suburbs (e.g. Richmond, Chelsea, Kensington) have lower mortality and morbidity than poorer suburbs (e.g. Tower Hamlets, Haringey).

10 Differences in health in the UK are related to factors such as poverty (e.g. income), poor housing, inadequate education, unemployment, drug abuse etc.

11 In areas of low population density (e.g. remote rural areas) healthcare services will be widely scattered and residents often have to travel long distances to access them.

12 Old people and people with low incomes have limited mobility (i.e. they lack personal transport). In rural areas, with limited public transport provision, accessing healthcare may be problematic for these groups.

13 Opportunities for exercise may be limited by a lack of facilities (e.g. gyms, swimming pools) and high crime rates (i.e. it may be unsafe to exercise outdoors).

14 In low income neighbourhoods in cities there may be few retailers selling fresh food; in rural areas choice of food shops is also limited; low income groups cannot afford higher-cost, healthy foods such as fresh fruit and vegetables.

15 South Lakeland has an ageing population. The proportion of residents aged 65+ years is well above the national average. The incidence of degenerative diseases (cancer, cardio-vascular, dementia) and morbidity is high, and will rise in future putting huge pressures on healthcare services.

Check your understanding

1 HIV/AIDS is concentrated in the economically less developed world and in sub-Saharan Africa (e.g. countries such as South Africa, Botswana, Namibia, etc.). Diabetes, because it is associated with obesity, is disproportionately concentrated in the economically developed world (e.g. North America, Europe).

2 Cuba, a middle-income country, has a highly effective healthcare system, which comprises primary and secondary services, an emphasis on preventative medicine, and is generously staffed with doctors. It is also free. Cubans have a long life expectancy. Haiti is a low-income country. Poverty and poor governance result in only a rudimentary healthcare system. Little priority and few resources are devoted to healthcare. There are severe shortages of doctors and medicines. There are few hospitals. The service relies heavily on charities and voluntary organisations. Mortality is high and life expectancy relatively low.

3 Regional inequalities in health in the UK are influenced by: poverty and income, lifestyles, housing, education, quality of healthcare offered by hospital trusts. Multiple deprivation, centred on low-income, is probably the principal factor determining geographical differences in health.

Chapter 9

Now test yourself

1 Primary data are original data collected through fieldwork or from primary (unpublished) sources. Secondary data are documents that have been processed and published.

2 Choropleth maps show spatial distributions by differences in colour or shading.

3 Isobars, isohyets, isotherms etc.

4 Continuous geographical distributions (e.g. pressure, temperature) are most effectively represented by isoline maps.

5 Charts may be used to represent data rather than tables because (a) they have greater visual appeal, (b) they show patterns and trends more clearly.

6 Triangular graphs could be used to show, among other things, soil texture (sand, silt, clay) and employment structure (primary, secondary, tertiary).

7 Logarithmic scales are used to present data with a wide range of values and convert a geometrical trend to a straight line.

8 The representativeness of the arithmetic mean can be compromised by extreme values in a data set.

9 An 'independent' variable causes change in another, so-called 'dependent' variable.

10 The coefficient of variation is used to compare variations of values in data sets that have means of different magnitudes.

11 (a) Perfect positive relationship = +1; (b) perfect inverse relationship = −1; (c) no relationship/random = around 0.

Check your understanding

1

2 Choropleth maps: use standardised data (densities), data are available for census units, easy to construct. However, distorted by variations in size of areal units, abrupt changes in values at boundaries misleading, choice of class boundaries subjective, could be large variations in density with areal units. Dot maps: absolute data values needed, clustering dots gives clear indication of densities, placement of dots is subjective, don't work well in areas of very low density. Isoline maps: location of isolines is highly subjective, difficult to draw in isolines.

3 Measures of central tendency summarise a data set with a single, representative, central value. Measures of dispersion provide an indication of the spread or range of values in a data set.

4 Statistical significance is the likelihood that the result of an investigation could have occurred by chance. If the likelihood is 5% or less, the result is normally accepted as statistically significant. Statistical significance is important in geography where so many investigations are based on samples and researchers must have confidence in their results.